KNITTING
KNOW-HOW

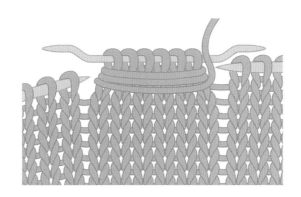

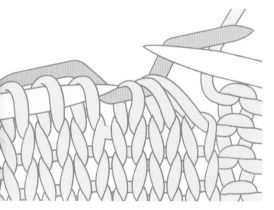
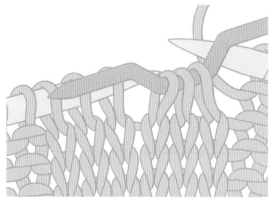
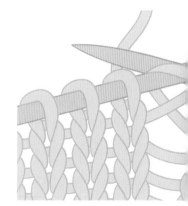

KNITTING KNOW-HOW

TECHNIQUES AND TIPS FOR ALL LEVELS OF SKILL FROM BEGINNER TO ADVANCED

CICO BOOKS

LONDON NEW YORK

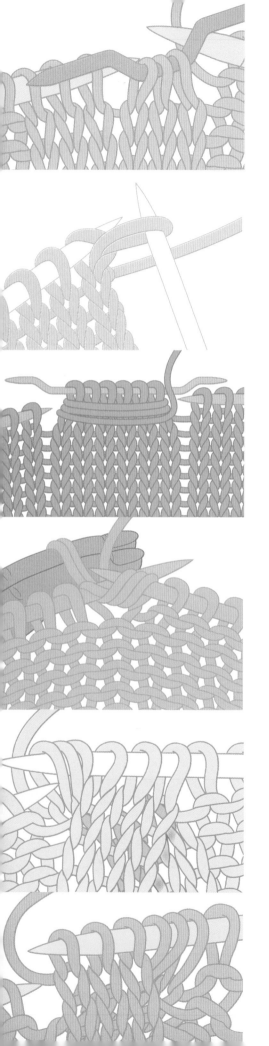

Published in 2020 by CICO Books
An imprint of Ryland Peters & Small Ltd
20–21 Jockey's Fields   341 E 116th St
London WC1R 4BW   New York, NY 10029

www.rylandpeters.com

10 9 8 7 6 5 4 3 2 1

Text, design, and illustrations © CICO Books 2020

A CIP catalog record for this book is available from the
Library of Congress and the British Library.

ISBN: 978-1-78249-827-8

Printed in China

Editor: Marie Clayton
Illustrator: Stephen Dew

Art director: Sally Powell
Production manager: Gordana Simakovic
Publishing manager: Penny Craig
Publisher: Cindy Richards

contents

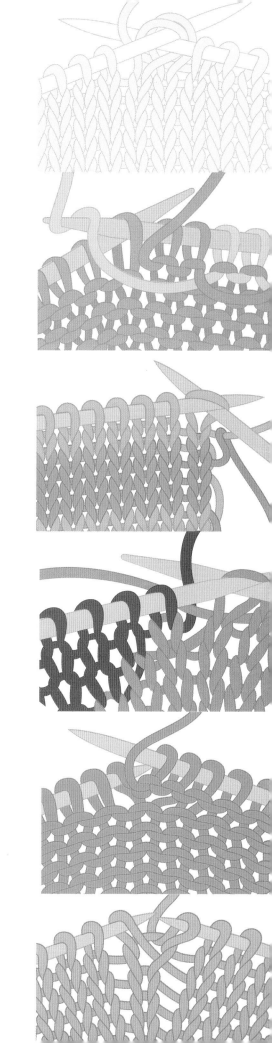

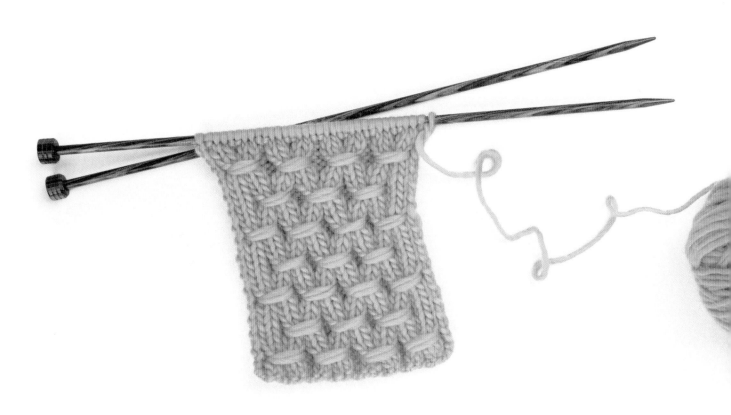

introduction

However experienced a knitter you are, every now and then there will be a technique that you are unfamiliar with, or just haven't used for a while. If you are a beginner, you may just need help remembering the simple knit and purl stitches, or working out which way of holding the yarn works best for you.

Whatever your level of skill, this comprehensive guide to knitting techniques will be an invaluable resource. Each area of knitting, from casting on to blocking and sewing up seams, is covered in detail, with step-by-step instructions and clear artworks to help you learn new skills as well as brush up on old ones.

Useful charts of needle sizes and pattern abbreviations, plus lots
of information about the different types and weights of yarn and
the fibers they are made of, can be referred to time and again.
There's even a list of all the equipment you will need, and tips
on reading patterns and charts. But to get started, you'll just
need some needles, some yarn, and some knitting know-how.

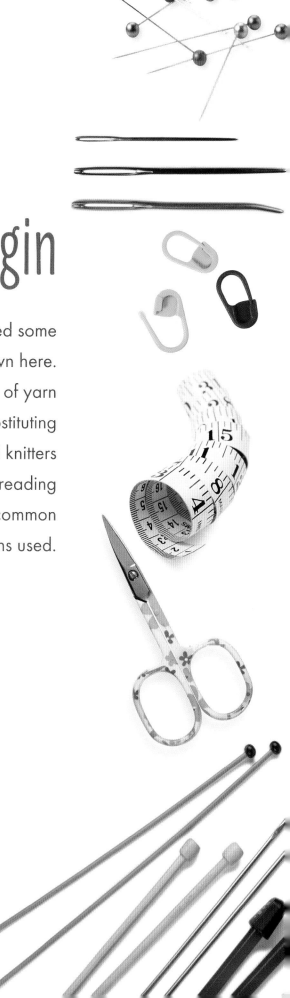

before you begin

If you are a beginner, you will need some basic equipment as shown here. The different varieties and weights of yarn are described, along with tips on substituting yarn, for beginners and experienced knitters alike. There's also a quick guide to reading patterns, including the common abbreviations used.

EQUIPMENT

To get started on a piece of knitting the only pieces of equipment you need are just needles, a yarn needle for sewing in ends, and scissors to cut the yarn. However, there are a few other items that will make your work easier.

NEEDLES

Knitting needles are available in plastic, metal, wood, and bamboo. Some people find metal needles harder on the hands, particularly those who suffer from arthritis. Bamboo and wood are said to help with this, although they can be more expensive.

Needles come in many sizes: US size 0 (2 mm) is the smallest standard size and is very thin indeed, but needles go up to US size 50 (25 mm) and beyond for knitting with super-thick yarns or fabric strips. The most commonly used sizes, however, range from US size 3 (3.25 mm) for fingering (4-ply) yarn up to US size 10½ (6.5 mm) for bulky (chunky) yarn. US size 6 (4 mm) needles and a light worsted (DK) yarn is a good starting combination to learn with.

Straight needles come in various lengths—if you find it comfortable to knit lower on your body, with your needles toward your lap, then 12-in. (30-cm) long needles may be better for you, 14-in. (35-cm) long needles are useful for any style of knitting, and 16-in. (40-cm) needles are better for those who knit with one needle under one arm.

As well as straight needles there are circular needles, used for knitting in the round and frequently employed for knitting necklines and collars. These needles have a pair of shorter needle points connected by a length of nylon cord, and they are available in the same range of sizes as straight needles and a variety of cord lengths. For more guidance about knitting with circular needles, see page 30.

Finally, there are sets of double-pointed needles, also known as "dpns." As the name implies, these have pointed tips at both ends and are used for specialist knitting, usually in the round for small tubular projects such as socks or gloves. See page 31 for guidance on working with dpns.

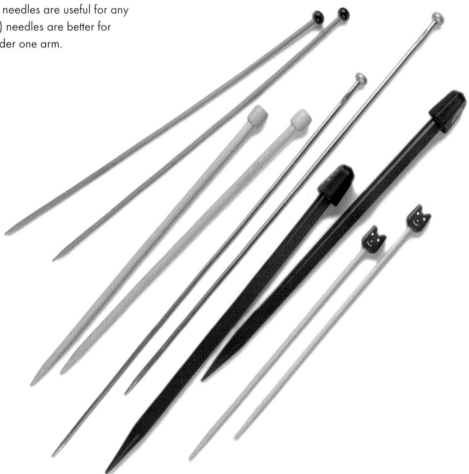

DOUBLE-POINTED AND CIRCULAR NEEDLES

Double-pointed needles usually come in sets of four and it's a good idea to keep them in their pocket or tied together, as otherwise it's easy to lose one. Circular needles come in different lengths; use the length specified in the pattern—if the cord is too long or too short for the number of stitches, it can cause problems. Circular needles can also be used for knitting back and forth in rows on very large projects such as shawls and afghans.

NEEDLE SIZE CONVERSION CHART

UK/European and US needle sizes are differently labeled. If you have some very old needles, perhaps passed down from family members, they may have an older numbering system, so use the conversion chart below or a needle gauge—which has labeled holes for all the common needle sizes—to work out the modern equivalent size.

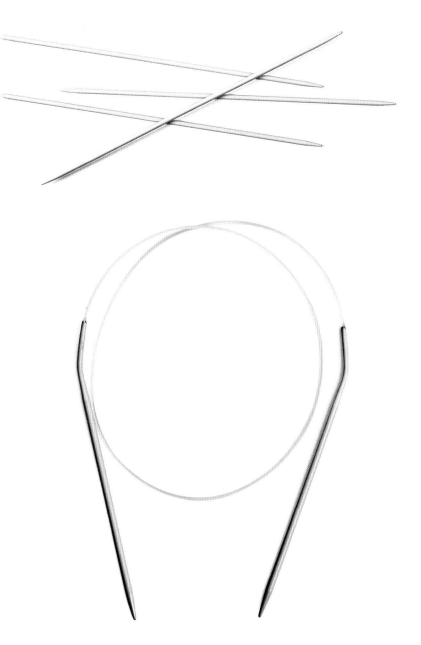

US size	Metric size (mm)	Old UK/ Canadian
0	2.0	14
1	2.25	13
2	2.75	12
–	3.0	11
3	3.25	10
4	3.5	–
5	3.75	9
6	4.0	8
7	4.5	7
8	5.0	6
9	5.5	5
10	6.0	4
10½	6.5	3
–	7.0	2
–	7.5	1
11	8.0	0
13	9.0	00
15	10.0	000
17	12.0	–
19	16.0	–
35	19.0	–
50	25.0	–

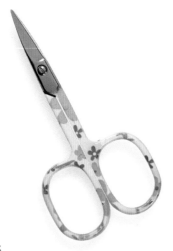

SHARP SCISSORS

Reserved for cutting yarn and thread only: do not cut paper with these, as it will blunt them.

TAPE MEASURE

A tape with both inches and millimeters is ideal, so that you can convert measurements in the pattern if necessary.

PINS

Rustproof, glass-headed, or T-headed quilters' pins to pin knitted pieces together. Bright-colored tops will help to avoid the pins getting lost in the knitted fabric.

STITCH MARKERS

Little rings that slip on to the needles or through a stitch to mark the start of rounds, or a particular place in the knitting.

STITCH HOLDERS

These are clips with a horizontal bar that you slip groups of stitches onto, and then clip closed, in order to save the stitches for later use (see page 65).

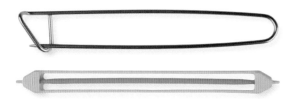

YARN NEEDLE

The blunt end will not split the yarn when sewing up and the large eye makes it easier to thread with yarn.

CABLE NEEDLE

A small, double-pointed knitting needle for holding stitches when creating cable patterns (see page 48).

ROW COUNTER

This is a small, tubular counter that fits on the end of your knitting needle; you click it round after each row.

CROCHET HOOK

You may sometimes need a crochet hook for decorative edgings (see page 94) or to pick up stitches (see page 66).

YARN

When it comes to yarn, it helps to have some information about all the different options that are available. Using the right yarn with the correct needles will make the knitting process much easier and will help to ensure that the items you make will look good and be the right size.

A vast array of knitting yarns is on offer, and the number will only increase as new materials are invented. Your pattern should guide you as to what type and thickness of yarn to use, but if you do not have a pattern then the chart below will help you match yarn thickness to needle size.

When choosing a yarn, consider the purpose of the item. Children loathe scratchy sweaters so you would not choose rough wool for a baby jacket—something soft such as a cotton blend, soft acrylic, bamboo, or silk blend would produce a

snuggly fabric. Similarly, soft cotton would not be suitable for formal socks because cotton has no elasticity and would soon become baggy—a specialist wool and nylon sock yarn has durability and stretch, making it a much better choice.

If you need to find a yarn substitute you need one with the same recommended needle size, as shown on the chart on page 11, and gauge (tension)—stitches and rows per 4 in./10 cm—which will be indicated in the pattern itself.

STANDARD YARN WEIGHT
Categories of yarn, gauge (tension) ranges, and recommended knitting needle sizes

Yarn weight symbol & category names	LACE [0]	SUPER FINE [1]	FINE [2]	LIGHT [3]	MEDIUM [4]	BULKY [5]	SUPER BULKY [6]
Types of yarns* in category	10-count crochet thread, US fingering	UK 4-ply sock, baby, US fingering	baby, US sport	DK, US light worsted	US worsted, afghan, Aran	craft, rug, chunky	bulky, roving, UK super chunky
Gauge (tension) in stockinette (stocking) stitch to 4 in. (10 cm)	33–40** sts	27–32 sts	23–26 sts	21–24 sts	16–20 sts	12–15 sts	6–11 sts
Recommended needle in metric size range	1.5–2.25 mm	2.25–3.25 mm	3.25–3.75 mm	3.75–4.5 mm	4.5–5.5 mm	5.5–8 mm	8 mm and larger
Recommended needle in US size range	001 to 1	1 to 3	3 to 5	5 to 7	7 to 9	9 to 11	11 and larger

*   The generic yarn-weight names in the yarn categories include those commonly used in the UK and US.

** Ultra-fine lace-weight yarns are difficult to put into gauge ranges; always follow the gauge given in your pattern for these yarns.

FIBERS

There is a huge variety of yarns to choose from, made with all different types of fibers. Here are some of the more common types.

THE NATURALS
100% wool

If a yarn is marked as "100% wool," this means that it has 100% animal content of some kind, usually sheep. If the ball band says merino, this comes from the Merino breed of sheep, well known for its fine soft fiber content. Other breeds of sheep also produce soft yarns, for example Blue Faced Leicester, which is a British breed.

Alpaca

Alpaca yarns are mainly mixed with merino yarns, typically 50:50. Alpaca is a natural fiber that comes from the animal of the same name. Depending on how it is spun, alpaca yarn can be either heavy or light and is available in a variety of thicknesses. It is soft, warmer than sheep's wool and has no lanolin, which makes it hypoallergenic.

Cashmere

A very soft and silky fiber, which comes from the undercoat of goats and is a hair rather than a fleece. It's a very warm and fine fiber usually spun into a fine yarn. Cashmere is often used in a mix with wool because a ball of 100% cashmere yarn is very expensive.

Cotton

A natural fiber, cotton comes in all thicknesses, starting with the finest threads. It was very popular several years ago when finely spun cottons were knitted up into garments and home accessories. Recently produced cottons are spun considerably thicker and are often good for summer projects. Cotton is often mixed with acrylics and wool, which make it into a softer yarn.

Mohair

Mohair is a "hairy," silky fiber that is made from the hair of the Angora goat. It is often used with a mix of silk and wool. It dyes very well and the colors are often vibrant. It's more expensive than wool fibers and is spun fine, although the long hair fibers knit as a dense and warm fabric and can be used with comparatively large needles.

Bamboo

Bamboo yarn is a very soft yarn and is produced, as its name implies, from bamboo fibers. It's often mixed with cotton or with other fibers.

THE SYNTHETICS
Acrylic

Acrylic yarn is synthetic and is manufactured to imitate wool yarn. Its appeal is that it is a cheaper fiber than wool. It is often mixed with wool to create a more economic yarn, while retaining some of the warmth properties of pure wool. Aside from the cost advantage, the other advantage is that many acrylic yarns can be put in the washing machine.

FANCY YARNS

"Fancy" yarn is a general term and it covers anything that might be fashionable. Fancy yarns are generally made of a mix of acrylics and can be "hairy" with a touch of shimmer from added lurex, sequins, or glitter.

There are also ribbon yarns, which are fabric strips of ribbon that are wound into balls.

You can also buy balls of fabric strips. These are often used for large projects worked on an extra-large needle or for arm knitting. They are ideal for making rugs and seat cushions.

Cotton light worsted/DK 100% cotton
125 yd (115 m) per 1¾oz 50g) ball

22 sts and 30 rows per 4 in. (10 cm) over st st
using US size 6 (4mm) knitting needles.
705 Pale Blue – Dye lot 7836

Made in Turkey
www.lordyarns.com

LOOKING AT YARN LABELS

When buying yarn you might shop in person at a local yarn store, department store, or craft fair, or you might prefer to shop online, where you can sometimes find a really good deal and a huge range but can't actually feel the yarn. Whichever you opt for, there should be standard information on either the ball band of the yarn or–if you are shopping online–on the web page, which will help you choose the type and quantity to buy.

- Brand: the name of the company that produced the yarn.
- Fiber content: such as "55% wool/45% silk."
- Yardage/meterage: this tells you the length of yarn in one ball or hank. This is particularly important when substituting yarn, because your alternative may hold less or more yarn per ball so you might need more or fewer balls than the pattern states.
- Aftercare instructions: you will often find guidance on how to wash and dry the completed garment.
- Washing instructions: washing symbols are usually included on the yarn label to tell you how to care for your finished make.

- Needle size: the recommended size for best results–you might see either the size or a suggested range.
- Gauge (tension) guide: a suggestion of how many stitches and rows per 4 in. (10 cm) should be achieved by the "average" knitter, using the needle size given.
- Dye lot number: this indicates which dye batch the yarn comes from. The color can vary between batches, so for one-color items it's best to buy all the yarn from the same dye lot.

SUBSTITUTING YARN

Patterns will indicate the yarn used. Either the pattern or the ball band of that yarn will give you the fiber content, weight and length per ball. The gauge (tension) you need to achieve on a particular stitch will be given in the pattern, and this may differ slightly from the standard gauge (tension) given on the ball band.

If you can't get the yarn specified in the pattern, or you want to use something from your stash, try and match all these elements as closely as possible, but in some cases an exact gauge (tension) match may not be possible. See page 28 for information on measuring gauge (tension). This may not matter much on smaller makes, but for a larger project or a shaped garment it could be a problem.

If the length per ball of your substitute yarn is different to the original yarn, you will need to work out the total length needed by multiplying the number of balls required by the length per ball of the original yarn, then dividing that total by the number of yards/meters per ball in your chosen yarn.

READING A PATTERN

Knitting patterns follow a similar formula, and use abbreviations for common terms. Once you are used to the format of knitting patterns you will find that they become very familiar and will give the following information:

Materials: what yarn to use, how much to buy for each size, (using brackets if applicable, see Sizing below), what size needles to use, any extra notions (haberdashery items) such as buttons, and extra equipment such as cable needles, stitch holders, etc.

Sizing: Actual measurements of the finished piece and, in the case of garments, the measurements on the body they are intended to fit. Several sizes might be given in brackets; for example small(medium:large), so if you are following the medium size, use the information that comes first inside each set of brackets.

Gauge (tension): The number of stitches and rows to 4 in. (10 cm) when working a given pattern on the recommended needles. If you do not work to the stated gauge (tension) your piece will not be the given size, and garments may fit oddly or not at all.

Abbreviations: Details of what the abbreviations used in the pattern mean. These are usually standard (see right), but there may also be some special abbreviations that are only applicable to that pattern.

In addition there may also be one or more charts for color work or showing a texture pattern, with a key alongside to explain the symbols/colors used. Charts may show an entire garment piece or just a section, and should have markers along the bottom and side to help you count rows and stitches. See pages 78, 80, and 81 for more information about charts.

If you are making a garment or a complex piece you may also see a schematic diagram—either an outline showing the actual measurements at various points, or an assembly diagram.

alt	alternat(e)ing
approx	approximately
beg	begin(ning)
C	cable
cont	continu(e)ing
cm	centimeter(s)
dec	decrease
dpn	double-pointed needle
foll	follow(ing)
in	inch(es)
inc	increase
inc 1	inc by knitting twice into stitch
k	knit
k2tog	knit two stitches together
LH	left hand
M1	make 1 stitch increase
MB	make bobble
p	purl
p2tog	purl two stitches together
patt	pattern
pm	place marker
psso	pass slipped stitch(es) over stitch just knitted
rem	remain(ing)
rep	repeat
RH	right hand
RS	right side
sl	slip
ssk	slip 1 stitch, slip 1 stitch, knit the 2 slipped stitches together
st st	stockinette (stocking) stitch
st(s)	stitch(es)
tbl	through the back loop
tog	together
WS	wrong side
yf/yfwd	yarn forward
yo	yarn over the needle
yrn	yarn wrapped around the needle
[ ]	work instructions within brackets as many times as directed
*/**	work instructions after/between asterisks as directed

basic skills

Knitted fabric consists of a series of rows or rounds, with the yarn looping in and out of the previous row or round of loops. As the very first step you will need to know how to hold the yarn and the needles, how to start off the knitting, known as casting on, and how to finish it off securely, so that it does not unravel, known as binding (or casting) off. This section also covers making a swatch to check you are working to the correct gauge (tension).

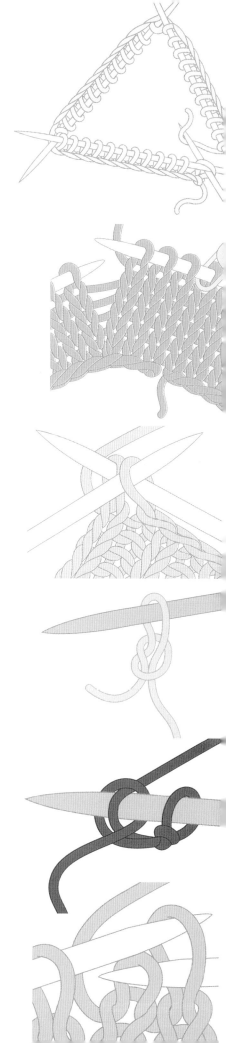

HOLDING THE NEEDLES

If you are a knitting novice, you will need to work out which is the most comfortable way for you to hold your needles.

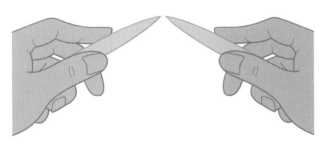 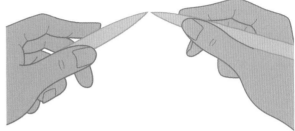

LIKE A KNIFE

Pick up the needles, one in each hand, as if you were holding a knife and fork—that is to say, with your hand lightly over the top of each needle. As you knit, you will tuck the blunt end of the right-hand needle under your arm, let go with your hand, and use your hand to mainpulate the yarn, returning your hand to the needle to move the stitches along.

LIKE A PEN

Now try changing the right hand so you are holding the needle as you would hold a pen, with your thumb and forefinger lighlty gripping the needle close to its pointed tip and the shaft resting in the crook of your thumb. As you knit, you will not need to let go of the needle but simply slide your right hand forward to manipulate the yarn.

Positioning the fingers

Try to keep your stitches and your fingertips close to the tips of the needles when you are working: this is much more efficient, because it means that your fingers and hands don't move as much for each stitch, which reduces the strain on your hands.

Some people like to keep one needle fixed, by tucking it under their right arm so that the right hand can concentrate on just working with the yarn. The left needle is held like a pen and moves as normal. This does give a lot of control but is not for everyone, although you may find it comfortable. It is common practice in the North of England and Scotland, and in some parts of Europe.

HOLDING THE YARN

As you knit, you will be working stitches off the left-hand needle and on to the right needle, and the yarn you are working with needs to be tensioned and manipulated to produce an even fabric. To hold and tension the yarn, you can use either your right or left hand, depending on the method you are going to use to make the stitches.

YARN IN RIGHT HAND

To knit and purl in the US/UK style (see pages 34 and 36), hold the yarn in your right hand. There are two ways of doing this.

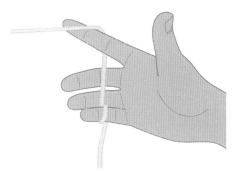

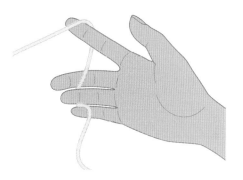

To hold the yarn tightly, wind it right around your little finger, under your ring and middle fingers, then pass it over your index finger, which will manipulate the yarn.

For a looser hold, catch the yarn between your little and ring fingers, pass it under your middle finger, then over your index finger.

YARN IN LEFT HAND

To knit and purl in the Continental style (see pages 34 and 37), hold the yarn in your left hand. This method is also sometimes easier for left-handed people to use..

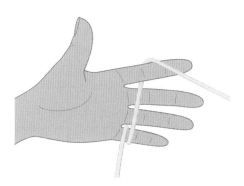

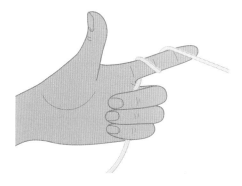

To hold the yarn tightly, wind it right around your little finger, under your ring and middle fingers, then pass it over your index finger, which will manipulate the yarn.

For a looser hold, fold your little, ring, and middle fingers over the yarn, and wind it twice around your index finger.

CASTING ON

There are many, many ways to cast on stitches. Some methods give a particular quality to the edge of the work: they are either more elastic, so suited to things like stretchy cuffs, or give a rigid edge that is firm with added strength.

MAKING A SLIPKNOT
A slipknot is the first loop that you put onto the needle to begin casting on in knitting.

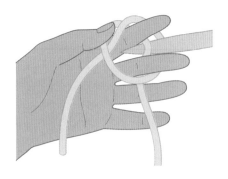 

1 Make a slipknot by winding the yarn twice around the first two fingers of your left hand, then bend these fingers forward. Draw the rear thread through the front one to form a loop.

2 With the knitting needle in your right hand, slide the loop onto the needle. Remove your fingers, then pull the two ends to tighten the loop on the needle and create the first stitch. Keep the needle with the slipknot in your left hand.

Which cast on to use

• The cable cast on is a good all-rounder; it is firm, durable, even, and neat, but makes a less elastic edge. It is easy for beginners.

• The thumb cast on is easy, quick and elastic, so great when stretch is needed. It's good to use on garter stitch pieces.

• The long tail cast on is quick and intuitive once learned, and produces a neat even edge. It is prone to being tight, in which case use two needles held together in the right hand and discard one when the cast on is complete.

• The magic loop cast on is great when working small projects in the round, and for using a circular needle of any length instead of double-pointed needles.

CABLE METHOD

This method makes a firm edge and uses two needles. It is given for the English method of knitting here.

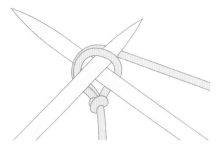

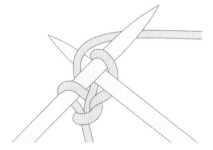

1 First make a slipknot (see opposite). Keep the yarn at the back and insert the right needle into the slipknot, from front to back, as shown in the illustration. Wrap the yarn from the ball end round the tip of the right needle and pull downward gently on it.

2 Draw the tip of the right needle through the loop and, as you do so, nudge the yarn through the loop of the slip knot to make a new loop. Turn the needle a little and slip this new loop onto the left needle, in front of the slip knot, and off the right needle. You now have 2 stitches.

3 Now insert the tip of the right needle between the two stitches on the left needle. Wrap the yarn over the right needle, from left to right. Now draw the yarn through to form a loop as you did before, then transfer it to the left needle and off the right, as you did in step 2.

Repeat step 3 until you have created the desired number of stitches.

THUMB CAST ON

Many knitters think this is the easiest way to cast on. It involves knitting into a loop made around the thumb to make a stitch on the needle. Leave a long tail of about ¾ in. (2 cm) per stitch to be cast on and then make a slip knot; the slip knot will be the first stitch.

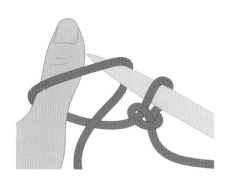

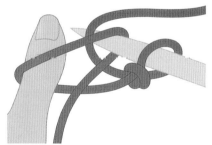

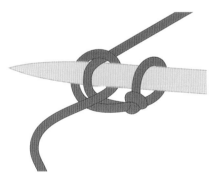

1 Holding the needle and the yarn from the ball in your right hand, use the free tail of yarn to make a loop around your left thumb while at the same time keeping the yarn taut between the third and fourth fingers of your left hand. Insert the needle tip into the loop.

2 Bring the yarn from the ball up between your thumb and the needle then take it around the needle, as shown above.

3 Draw the yarn through to make a stitch on the needle, then release the loop from the left thumb and gently pull on the yarn tail to tighten the stitch on the needle.

LONG TAIL CAST ON

Another method that only uses one needle plus finger and thumb, this might look hard to understand at first glance. However, once you get the hang of it, it will become intuitive and relatively quick to work. It produces a neat, even edge that is suitable for projects that begin with a section of ribbing.

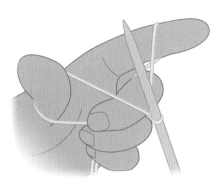

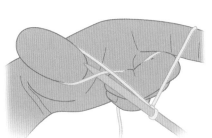

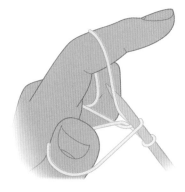

1 Pull out a long tail of yarn, then make a slip knot and put it onto a needle, holding this needle in your dominant hand. Hold your other hand with the palm facing toward you, and wind the long tail of yarn around your thumb in a counterclockwise direction. Pass the other end of the yarn (attached to the ball) over your index finger, as shown. Trap both the strands in place under your third and little finger.

2 Insert your needle under the horizontal strand of yarn that is on the outside of your thumb.

3 Now guide the needle over and then under the strand attached to your index finger, as shown.

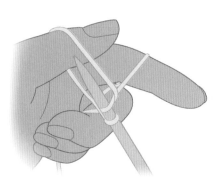

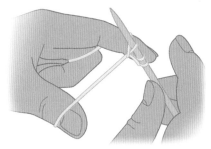

4 Bring the needle back through the center of the loop around your thumb to make the stitch.

5 Remove your thumb from the loop and tighten up the stitch by pulling on the long tail. Reposition the yarn around your thumb, as in step 1, and repeat these steps for each cast on stitch.

BACKWARD LOOP CAST ON

This is a quick and easy method of casting on stitches, often used to cast on stitches for armholes and for the thumb of fingerless mittens. It's shown here worked after a slipknot, but the method is the same if the stitches are being cast on after an existing knitted stitch.

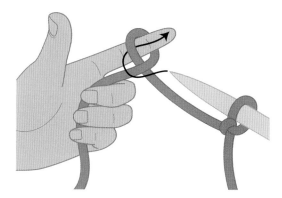

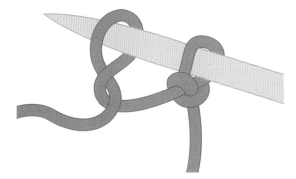

1 Hold the knitting needle in your right hand. *From front to back, wrap the working yarn around your left index finger. Slip the needle under the loop around your finger in the direction indicated by the arrow.

2 Slide your thumb out of the loop and pull the new stitch tight on the needle. Repeat from * until you have cast on the required number of stitches.

MAGIC LOOP CAST ON

A more recent technique, this is a useful cast on for circular projects. You will need a circular needle—this is an innovative way of working a smaller project on a circular needle that theoretically should be too big for it, thus avoiding the use of dpns.

Using the circular needle, cast on the required number of stitches. Divide in half and slide one half onto the cord of the needle and the other half onto the left needle tip. Pull the length of the cord through the gap between the two lots of stitches, making a loop between them. Make sure the stitches are not twisted and all still have their base hanging at the bottom. Place a stitch marker at the start of the round. Pull the right needle tip away from the stitches, so that they slide back onto the cord, and use this tip as the working needle. Knit stitches off the left-hand needle tip as normal, pulling tightly on the first couple of stitches to make sure that the round closes seamlessly. You now have stitches on the right-hand needle tip and on the cord, but none on the left-hand needle tip. Slide the stitches on the cord onto the left-hand needle tip, and those that are on the right-hand needle tip onto the cord, then knit off the left-hand needle tip in the same way. Continue to knit rounds in the same way, remembering to move the stitch marker up on every row.

BINDING (CASTING) OFF

Once you've finished knitting a piece, you need to bind (cast) off the stitches to prevent the knitting unraveling. Normally you will do this knitwise (see page 34), but occasionally you may be instructed to bind (cast) off purlwise (see page 36) or in pattern, such as ribbing (opposite).

 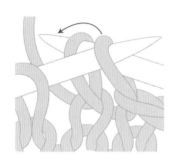 

1 Knit the first two stitches of the next row as usual. Insert the tip of the left needle into the first stitch worked on the right needle, from left to right and at the front of the work. Lift this stitch over the last stitch on the right needle, and drop it off the tip. You will have 1 stitch remaining on the right needle.

2 Knit one more stitch from the left needle as normal so that you again have 2 stitches on the right needle, then repeat step 1 again.

3 Repeat until you have only 1 stitch left on the right needle and none on the left needle. Pull a long loop of yarn, then remove the right needle, cut the yarn, and thread the end through the loop, tightening it to close.

Successful binding (casting) off

• Be aware of your gauge (tension)— see page 28—when binding (casting) off. If you work tightly the resulting edge with be quite firm and stable. For a more elastic edge, bind (cast) off loosely.

• It's also a good idea not to bind (cast) off too tightly if you will be picking up stitches (see page 66) along the edge later.

• If you need to work loosely but find it difficult to adjust your natural gauge (tension) try using a slightly larger needle to bind (cast) off..

• Unless your pattern instructs you otherwise, it's usually best to bind (cast) off with the right side of the work facing you.

BINDING (CASTING) OFF IN RIBBING

When you are working in a textural pattern it is good practice to bind (cast) off in the same way, maintaining the integrity of the pattern right up to the edge of the piece. Here is how to cast off in single ribbing (see page 38).

1 Place your needles as if you were about to start a new row. Knit the first stitch and purl the second one, as normal. Pass the yarn through to the back again, but do not knit the next stitch yet. Lift the first stitch over the last stitch on the right needle, and off the right needle, as for regular binding (casting) off. You will then have one stitch remaining on the right needle.

2 Repeat step 1, working the stitches on the left needle in ribbing, then binding (casting) them off as normal, until you have no more left on the left needle and only two on the right needle. Lift the first of these over the last, then cut the yarn and thread the loose tail through the remaining stitch to finish. Pull to close and then weave in the loose end.

You should always aim to bind (cast) off in ribbing when you have just been knitting in ribbing, but follow the same pattern of ribbing you have been working, knitting the knit stitches and purling the purl stitches, then lifting the stitches over as for a regular bind (cast) off.

GAUGE (TENSION)

Gauge (tension) is one of the most important aspects of successful knitting—it refers to the tightness of a knitted fabric.

You need to match your gauge (tension) to that given in the pattern you are working on so that your version of the item comes out the same size. This might sound hard to achieve, but all you need to know is how to make a gauge (tension) swatch, how to measure it, and what adjustments to make if your gauge (tension) does not match that in the pattern. This is even more crucial when you use a different yarn from that suggested in the pattern.

The gauge (tension) in a knitting pattern, or on the ball band of yarn, is given as "X sts and Y rows to 4 in. (10 cm)." In a pattern it might also say "over pattern on US size XX (XX mm) needles," but if no stitch pattern is given it means it is worked in stockinette (stocking) stitch.

Making sample swatches might seem a tedious process but it really is vital—even a small variation in gauge (tension) could produce a big difference in size over a larger piece—

over-long sleeves, too short sweaters, or sagging shoulders can all be the product of incorrect gauge (tension). When you intend to invest your time and attention in knitting a piece, it's worth making sure it starts off right.

MAKING A GAUGE (TENSION) SWATCH

A gauge (tension) is given with each pattern to help you make your project the same size as the sample. The gauge is given as the number of stitches and rows you need to work to produce a 4-in (10-cm) square of knitting.

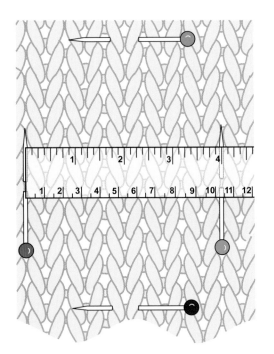

Using the recommended yarn and needles, cast on 8 stitches more than the gauge (tension) instruction asks for—so if you need to have 10 stitches to 4in (10cm), cast on 18 stitches. Working in the pattern as instructed, work 8 rows more than are needed. Bind (cast) off loosely.

Lay the swatch flat without stretching it. Lay a ruler across the stitches as shown, with the 2in (5cm) mark centered on the knitting, then put a pin in the knitting at the start of the ruler and at the 4in (10cm) mark: the pins should be well away from the edges of the swatch. Count the number of stitches between the pins. Repeat the process across the rows to count the number of rows to 4in (10cm).

If the number of stitches and rows you've counted is the same as the number asked for in the instructions, you have the correct gauge (tension). If you do not have the same number then you will need to change your gauge (tension).

To change gauge (tension) you need to change the size of your knitting needles. A good rule of thumb to follow is that one difference in needle size will create a difference of one stitch in the gauge (tension). You will need to use larger needles to achieve fewer stitches, and smaller ones to achieve more stitches.

ROWS AND ROUNDS

Knitting is often worked in rows, or sometimes in rounds, and almost always from right to left.

A row is a horizontal line of stitches that starts with the first stitch at one end and finishes with the last stitch at the other end. Knit the stitches from the left needle on to the right needle, until you come to the end. To continue working the next row, put the now full right needle in your left hand and the now empty needle in your right hand and work from the first stitch to the last again, and so on.

Knitting that is worked in rounds is always worked on the front, and on either circular needles (see page 30) or a set of double-pointed needles (see page 31).

For tips on counting rows or rounds in various stitches, see pages 35, 37, 38, and 40.

Using a stitch marker

As you work in the round, you should use a stitch marker to keep track of where each round starts. Placing a stitch marker at the beginning of the round will help you work out where you are in any given round should you lose your way. When you get to the end of the round, simply slide the marker from the left needle to the right on circular needles, or from the pin holding the next lot of stitches on to the free needle when using dpns.

Stitch markers are also useful when increasing and decreasing on straight needles, when you are not always knitting into the same stitch on each row.

KNITTING IN THE ROUND ON A CIRCULAR NEEDLE

First, make sure you have the right size needle (see gauge (tension) on page 28). Circular needles also come with different length cords, and your pattern may specify the length of cord you need as well, particularly if any of the pieces are very small or very large. If your cord is too long you may end up stretching the work to reach round to the other needle tip, and if the cord is too short you may not have room to hold all the stitches comfortably.

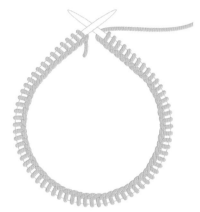

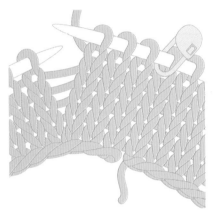

1 Cast on to one of the tips, sliding the stitches off onto the nylon cord as you go along, until you have the required number of stitches. Spread the stitches out along the length of the cord and tips evenly. Make sure all the stitches are facing the same way: check that the bases of the stitches are all sitting at the bottom all round. If they are not, twist them around until they are all sitting the same way. This is really important: if you do not check this carefully and a twist becomes knitted into your fabric from the first row onward, you will not be able to put it right without unraveling it all.

2 Now bring the ends of the circular needle together in front of you, so that the start of your cast-on row is at the tip of your left needle, and the end of it is at the tip of the right one. Keep the stitches all facing the right way, then place your stitch marker on the right needle and push it along so that it sits in front of the stitches. Insert the tip of the right needle into the first stitch on the left needle and begin the first round.

3 You can now keep knitting in the usual way, and you should notice that your knitting is joined in a circle. When you reach the stitch marker you have reached the end of the first round, so slip your stitch marker onto the right needle again, then begin Round 2.

KNITTING IN THE ROUND WITH DOUBLE-POINTED NEEDLES

If you do not have enough stitches to stretch round a circular needle, you will need to knit with a set of double-pointed needles (dpns). It is possible to knit with three, four, five, or even six double pointed needles, but the most common arrangement is to work on four. In each case stitches are distributed evenly over all needles except one, which functions as the working needle.

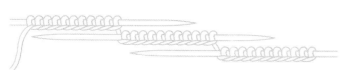

1 Divide evenly into three (if using four needles), or into four (if using five needles), the number of stitches you need to cast on. Here, a set of four needles is being used. Cast on (see page 22) to one needle one-third of the number of stitches needed, plus one extra stitch. Slip the extra stitch onto the second needle. Repeat the process, not forgetting to count the extra stitch, until the right number of stitches is cast on to each of the needles.

2 Arrange the needles in a triangle with the tips overlapping as shown here. As with circular needle knitting (see opposite) make sure that the cast-on edge is not twisted and place a round marker to keep track of the rounds. Pull the working tail of yarn across from the last stitch and using the free needle, knit the first stitch off the first needle, knitting it firmly and pulling the yarn tight. Knit the rest of the stitches on the first needle, which then becomes the free one, ready to knit the stitches off the second needle. Knit the stitches off each needle in turn; when you get back to the marker, you have completed one round. Slip the marker onto the next needle and knit the next round.

Using double-pointed needles

When you join the round, draw up the last stitch cast on as close as you can get it to the first cast-on stitch. This is to avoid an obvious join developing between the needles in the knitting, which will look like a ladder.

Hold the two working dpns like regular needles, in your left and right hands, and allow the needles currently not active to fall backward.

Each time you finish the stitches on a needle, rotate the work 90 degrees to work the next dpn. Then rotate again, and work the stitches off the following dpn. Continue in this way to the end.

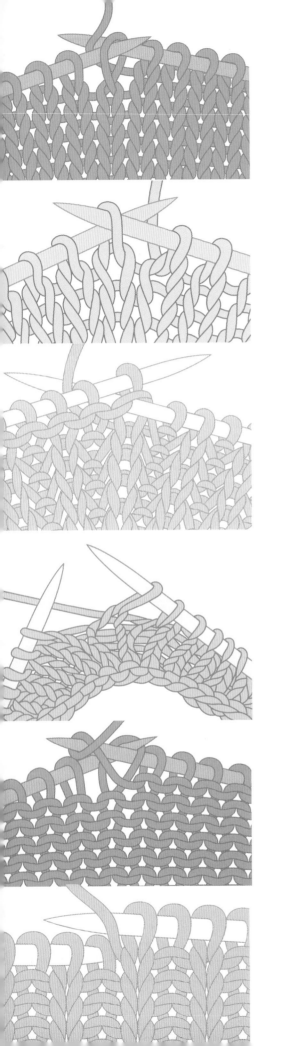

basic stitches

The basic stitches, and the building blocks of all knitted fabrics, are knit stitch (see page 34) and purl stitch (see page 36). These two stitches can be worked in a couple of different ways—choose the technique that feels most comfortable to you. Working these stitches in a sequence, or working into a different loop of the stitch or into the stitch in a row below, will create a different look to the knitted fabric.

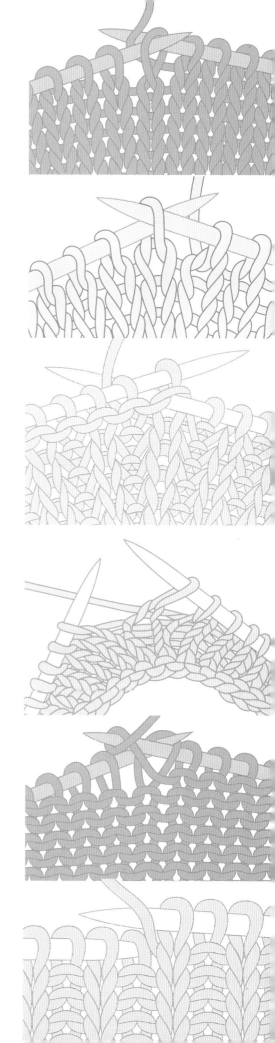

KNIT STITCH

There are only two stitches to master in knitting, and the knit stitch is the first one most people learn. In Europe and some other parts of the world, the method for making a stitch is called the English or American method, but you can also try the method known as Continental knitting and see which suits you best.

KNIT STITCH US/UK METHOD

Place the needle with the cast-on stitches in your left hand and the empty needle in your right. Thread your yarn around your right hand, as shown on page 21.

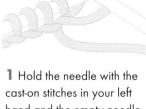

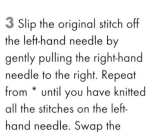

1 Hold the needle with the cast-on stitches in your left hand and the empty needle in your right hand. * From left to right, put the point of the right-hand needle into the front of the first stitch. Wrap the yarn around the point of the right-hand needle, again from left to right.

2 With the tip of the right-hand needle, pull the wrapped yarn through the stitch to form a loop. This loop is the new stitch.

3 Slip the original stitch off the left-hand needle by gently pulling the right-hand needle to the right. Repeat from * until you have knitted all the stitches on the left-hand needle. Swap the needles in your hands and you are ready to work the next row.

4 With the tip of the right needle, moving it to the right, push the stitch just worked off the tip of the left needle and gently tighten the new loop that now sits on the right needle. This is the first knit stitch. Repeat steps 1 to 4 for each stitch on the left needle, until this needle is empty.

KNIT STITCH CONTINENTAL METHOD

This is how to form a knit stitch if you are holding the yarn in your left hand and so working in the Continental style. If you are left-handed, you may find this method easier than the US/UK technique (see above).

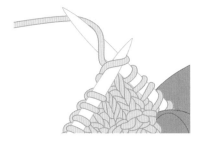
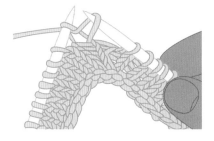
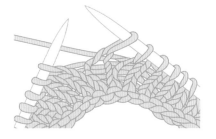

1 Hold the needle with the cast-on stitches in your left hand and the empty needle in your right hand. * From left to right, put the point of the right-hand needle into the front of the first stitch. Holding the working yarn fairly taut with your left hand at the back of the work, move the tip of the right-hand needle under the working yarn.

2 With the tip of the right-hand needle, bring the wrapped yarn through the stitch to form a loop. This loop is the new stitch.

3 Slip the original stitch off the left-hand needle by gently pulling the right-hand needle to the right. Repeat from * until you have knitted all the stitches on the left-hand needle. Swap the needles in your hands and you are ready to work the next row.

GARTER STITCH

The fabric you create when you knit every row is called garter stitch. It is quite a wide and thick fabric that lies flat and is fairly durable. It has characteristic ridges and looks exactly the same on both sides.

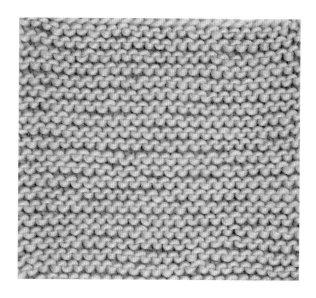

COUNTING ROWS AND STITCHES IN GARTER STITCH FABRIC

Knit stitches are formed by yarn snaking up and down and in and out of loops, in a zigzag fashion. It is useful to know how to count rows, so that you can keep track of where you are in a pattern.

If you look at the diagram on the left, you will notice that in garter stitch there is a wavy pattern, then a row of indented Vs above, before another wavy pattern. One wavy row and one indented row of Vs together represent two rows of garter stitch. So you can count the wavy rows upward in twos, and if at the very top of your work there is a row of indented Vs, that is another one row to add on.

It is a very good idea, especially when you are a beginner, to count your stitches on the needle at very regular intervals, to make sure you have not dropped any stitches or accidentally made any extra stitches. At this early stage, when you are still learning, do not worry too much about this: later workshops will show you how to put mistakes right, but for now try and notice any errors so that you can avoid making them again.

To count stitches on the needle, simply pick along the needle with your finger, moving the stitches along toward the tip a little (not too much, so that you don't stretch the stitches). Count in twos for speed.

To count the stitches along a row in garter stitch, each upper horizontal bar in the wavy line represents one stitch.

PURL STITCH

Purl is the other common stitch structure in knitting; essentially, purl is the same as a knit stitch, but worked from the reverse. So if you look at the reverse of a knit stitch you are looking at a purl stitch and vice versa (see opposite). Combining purl stitch and knit stitch in various ways will create stockinette (stocking) stitch, as well as many other textured stitches such as ribbing and seed (moss) stitch (see pages 38 and 40).

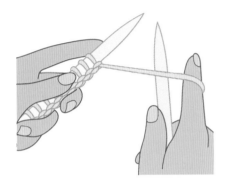

PURL STITCH US/UK METHOD

Place the needle with the cast-on stitches in your left hand and the empty needle in your right. Thread your yarn around your right hand, as shown on page 21.

1 At the start of the first row, instead of placing the working yarn behind the tip of the left needle—as you would to begin a knit row—bring it to the front of both needle tips as shown here.

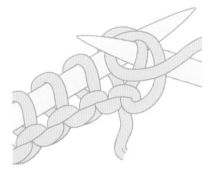

2 Insert the right needle into the front of the first stitch, from right to left. Wrap the yarn around the tip of the right needle, from right to left.

3 Pull the yarn through the stitch, to form a new stitch on the right needle.

4 Now slip the original stitch off the left needle by moving the right needle gently to the right. One purl stitch made.

Repeat steps 2 to 4 until you have worked all the stitches on the left needle. To continue, switch the needles over and start again with the full needle in your left hand.

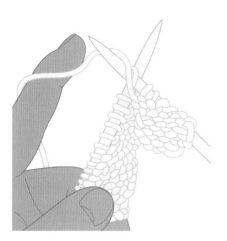

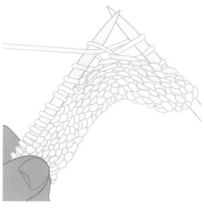

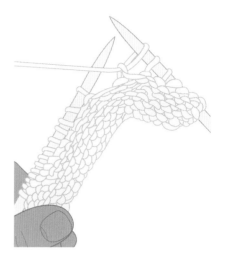

1 Place the needle containing all the stitches in your left hand and insert the tip of the right needle into the front of the first stitch, from right to left.

2 Hold the yarn at the back of the work, and keep it quite taut, but not tight. Pick up a loop of yarn with the tip of the right needle.

3 Use the tip of the right needle to draw this loop through the original stitch. This may feel trickier than making a knit stitch, but it is easy once you get used to the movements. Slip the original stitch off the left needle by moving the right needle gently to the right. Repeat steps 1 to 3 until all the stitches on the left needle have been used up.

STOCKINETTE (STOCKING) STITCH

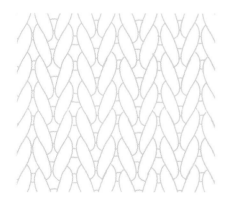

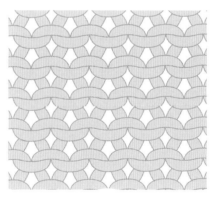

Stockinette (stocking) stitch is the most common knit structure—once you can identify it, you will spot it everywhere: your T-shirts, your sweatshirts, even your socks!

To create stockinette (stocking) stitch you work a row knitting every stitch and then in the next row you purl every stitch. Alternating these two rows makes a fabric with one very smooth side of V stitches and one more textured side of horizontal bars. The former is the knit side, the latter the purl side. As we mentioned earlier, the back of the knit-stitch row makes a purl row on the purl side (above left), and the back of the purl-stitch row forms a knit row on the knit side (above center). Try and follow the path of the yarn along one row with your finger: you will see that it is doing the same thing, but you are seeing it from either side.

To count rows in stockinette (stocking) stitch, you just count the V stitches in one vertical column on the right side of the work. To count stitches, count each V along a row.

RIBBING

The term ribbing describes a particular type of fabric with a regular pattern of alternating knit and purl stitches that is repeated every row. In order to make stockinette (stocking) stitch lie flat it is necessary to add a border or edging of another stitch structure, such as ribbing. Ribbing lies flat and is very stretchy—if you look at any sweater or pair of socks it is likely that you will spot some ribbing at the edges and it's useful for edging scarves, throws, and all manner of items. Ribbing has characteristically vertical ridges, which are usually the same width across the whole piece.

SINGLE RIBBING

A very basic ribbing structure is known as 1 x 1 or single ribbing, which means knit one stitch then purl one stitch repeated along the row.

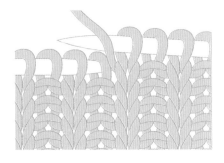 

1 Place the needle containing all the stitches in your left hand. Tension the yarn as usual, and begin by holding it at the back of the work and working a knit stitch into the first stitch. Now, bring the yarn through the gap between the two needle tips, so that it sits at the front of the work.

2 Work a purl stitch into the next stitch on the left needle. Then pass the yarn back through the gap between the two needle tips, to the back of the work, ready to work a knit stitch into the next stitch. After working the knit stitch, bring the yarn through the middle to the front and work a purl stitch—you should now have worked four stitches. Repeat this pattern of moving the yarn to the back then the front, and working a knit then a purl stitch, until you have worked all the stitches.

For the next row switch the needles so the full one is in your left hand. You finished the last row with a purl stitch, but now the reverse side is facing you so that last purl stitch will be worked as a knit stitch. So begin with a knit stitch and then alternate purl and knit across the row, again ending with a purl stitch.

RECOGNIZING DIFFERENT STITCHES

In stockinette (stocking) stitch (see page 37) you always knit the knit stitches, and purl the purl stitches. Look at your stockinette (stocking) stitch knitting, noting the difference in appearance between these two stitches. In ribbing you also knit the knit stitches and purl the purl stitches, so being able to tell which is which is really useful as you progress across the row.

To count rows in ribbing, count the number of V stitches in a vertical column. To count stitches, count each V stitch and horizontal bar in a row.

THE QUALITIES OF SINGLE RIBBING

Ribbing fabric has a distinctive appearance, with vertical lines of knit stitches (Vs) that are raised up, next to indented troughs of purl stitches; if you look closely you will notice the horizontal bars of the individual stitches. This ribbing pattern looks the same on both sides of the fabric.

When working on an even number of stitches every row will be the same, because each one starts on a knit stitch and ends on a purl stitch, so the knit side of the last stitch is facing ready to start with a knit stitch on the next row. With an odd number of stitches you start and end one row with a knit stitch, and start and end the next row with a purl stitch. You still work in the same way, but alternating these two rows.

You will also notice that, despite casting on a reasonable number of stitches, the ribbing fabric seems a lot narrower—this is typical of ribbing. If you pull the fabric horizontally it will expand out to the size cast on. Let it go and it will spring back. This elasticity is the most useful characteristic of ribbing, and is why it is so widely used in knitted fashion.

Additionally, ribbing is almost always worked in needles that are one or two sizes smaller than you would normally use. So, for example, if you are working in light worsted (DK) yarn and are making ribbing for the bottom of a sweater, you might use US size 3 (3.25 mm) needles for the ribbing sections, and (US size 6 (4 mm) needles for the stockinette (stocking) stitch main parts. This is because moving the yarn from back to front repeatedly between stitches when switching from knit to purl and vice versa adds to the stitch size and

decreases the elasticity, so going down a needle size or two compensates for this and maintains the properties of the ribbing.

For binding (casting) off in ribbing, see page 27. This is a very useful skill to learn. It will allow you to maintain the stretchy quality of your ribbing when it occurs at the end of a garment.

OTHER COMMON RIBBING VARIATIONS

You will encounter other variations of ribbing as your knitting skills increase. Some will have a completely regular pattern and will follow a similar formula; for example: knit two stitches, purl two stitches (written as k2, p2 and often known as 2 x 2 ribbing). This fabric looks the same on both sides.

Some will have a less regular pattern—for example, knit two stitches, purl one stitch (written as k2, p1 or 2 x 1 ribbing), or knit four stitches, purl two stitches (written as k4, p2). These more irregular patterns have a definite right (RS) and wrong side (WS) to the fabric, so take care to make sure you are working the RS pattern on the right side of your knitting, particularly if it occurs anywhere other than at the beginning of the work.

SEED (MOSS) STITCH

This is the simplest texture pattern, after ribbing (see page 38), and is worked in a very similar way. The difference is that in ribbing you knit every knit stitch and purl every purl stitch, but this pattern involves doing exactly the opposite. It is known as seed stitch in the USA and moss stitch in the UK.

If you are working on an even number of stitches:

Row 1: [K1, P1] to end.
Row 2: [P1, K1] to end.

If you cast on an odd number of stitches, then every row would be as Row 1 above, ending with a K1.

To make larger seed (moss) stitch, simply k2, p2 on the right side, and p2, k2 on the wrong side.

FISHERMAN'S RIB

This is a familiar variation on ribbing, which appears thicker and more pronounced in texture.

This effect is achieved by knitting into the row below (see below), rather than the working row. Always remember to slip (see opposite) the first stitch at the start of each row to avoid a wiggly, untidy edge.

COUNTING ROWS IN FISHERMAN'S RIBBING

Counting rows in this stitch pattern is not as straightforward as counting rows in regular ribbing because you have worked into the row below. Each large V represents two rows in this instance, so bear this in mind.

KNITTING INTO THE ROW BELOW

This is a technique you will need for Fisherman's ribbing.

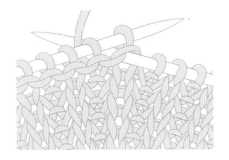

Insert the needle into the center of the knit stitch immediately below the one you would normally work next—in other words, one row below. Complete the knit stitch as normal.

SLIPPING STITCHES

Sometimes it is necessary to move a stitch from one needle to the other without working a stitch into it—this is known as slipping a stitch and is a very simple technique.

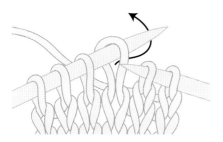

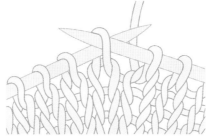

1 To slip a stitch knitwise, insert your right needle into the next stitch as if you were about to knit it, but instead of then wrapping the yarn, simply transfer the stitch off the left needle and onto the right one, without making a stitch. The yarn remains behind the work and is treated as normal for the following stitch.

2 To slip a stitch purlwise, insert your right needle into the next stitch as if you were about to purl it, with the yarn at the front unless otherwise instructed. Instead of wrapping the yarn, simply transfer the stitch off the left needle and onto the right one, without making a stitch.

THROUGH THE BACK LOOP

You usually knit or purl stitches by putting the right-hand needle into the front of the stitch. However, sometimes a stitch needs to be twisted to create an effect or to work a technique, and to do this you knit or purl into the back of it. This is called working "through the back loop" and is abbreviated to "tbl" in a knitting pattern.

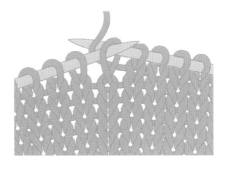

Knitting tbl

Put the right-hand needle into the back of the next stitch on the left-hand needle. Knit the stitch in the usual way (see page 34), but through the back loop.

Purling tbl

Put the right-hand needle into the next stitch on the left-hand needle. Purl the stitch in the usual way (see page 36), but through the back loop.

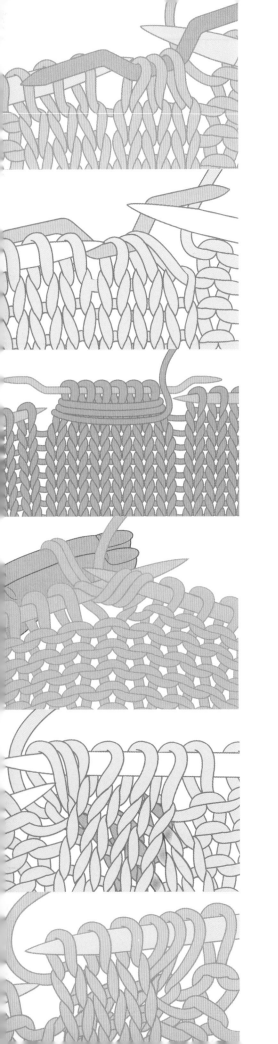

other stitches

This section contains some other stitch patterns to try that will add some interesting texture and different effects to the knitted fabric, ranging from bobbles and loops to cables and crossed stitches. All of these are easy to work and will add variety to your knitted pieces.

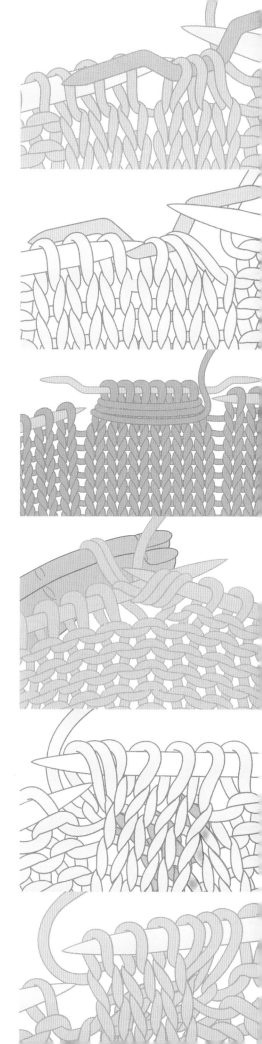

BOBBLES

Bobbles can be used as a textured pattern, and when worked in a contrast color they offer a very dramatic effect. They are a little fiddly to work, but after mastering the technique it is simply a matter of repetition.

WORKING A BOBBLE

A bobble is created by increasing several times into the same stitch, then decreasing in the following row.

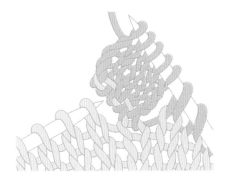

By increasing just once into a stitch, then decreasing in the following row, you will create a tiny indent of texture. Increasing more than once into the same stitch produces a larger physical area for the bobble. You can widen the increased area to include two or more stitches, and/or work several rows of short rowing (see page 70) over the increased stitches, before decreasing back to the original stitch, which will create a defined ridge or bobble.

LOOPS

To create a loopy fabric some dexterity is required, but once you have got used to looping the yarn around your thumb the rest is easy.

Insert the right needle into the next stitch on the left needle as if to knit as normal. Wrap the yarn around the needle and bring the right needle through as if knitting the stitch, but do not slip the loop off the needle. Open out the needles, and keeping your right thumb in the middle, bring the yarn over to the front wrapping it round your thumb, pass the yarn through to the back between the needles (the yarn is now wrapped round the thumb). Knit the stitch with the thumb still wrapped by yarn. Release the thumb from the strand of yarn to create the loop. Slip the first stitch over the second to secure the loop.

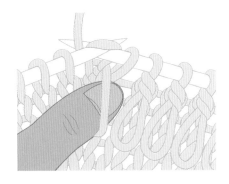

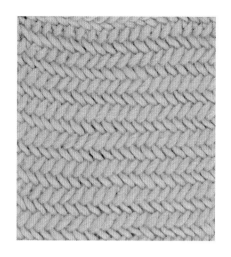

HERRINGBONE STITCH

For herringbone, each stitch—apart from the very first one in the row—is worked twice. The wrong-side rows are quite simple, but on the right-side rows the stitches are twisted before you knit them, which slows the process down. You twist the right-side row stitches using ssk (slip, slip, knit: see page 59), but only twist each stitch the first time you work it. It's a little complicated, but if you pick up needles and yarn and follow the instructions, it will make sense.

WRONG-SIDE ROW

Purl the first two stitches on the left-hand needle together, but only slip the first stitch off the left-hand needle. *Now, purl together the next two stitches—the stitch that has already been worked but left on the left-hand needle, and the next stitch—and again, just slip the first one off the left-hand needle. Rep from * until you have just one stitch left on the left-hand needle, then purl this stitch.

RIGHT-SIDE ROW

Slip the first stitch on the left-hand needle knitwise onto the right-hand needle, then slip the second stitch knitwise onto the right-hand needle. Insert the left-hand needle into the front of these two stitches and knit them together, but only slip the first stitch off the left-hand needle. *Now, put the right-hand needle into the front of the first stitch on the left-hand needle and slip it onto the right-hand needle, slip the second stitch knitwise onto the right-hand needle, insert the the left-hand needle into the front of these two stitches, and knit them together, but only slip the first stitch off the left-hand needle. Rep from * until you have just one stitch left on the left-hand needle, then knit this stitch.

BRIOCHE STITCH

This lovely stitch makes a wonderfully light and warm fabric. It's worked using stitches slipped purlwise (see page 41), with the yarn brought between the tips of the needles to the front of the work before slipping the stitch. After the stitch is slipped you make a yarn over (see page 61), so having the yarn at the front means it's already in the right position to make the yarn over.

FIRST ROW

*With the yarn held in front of the work, slip the first stitch purlwise, make a yarn over, then knit the next stitch. Rep from * to the end of the row.

EVERY FOLLOWING ROW

*With the yarn held in front of the work, slip the first stitch purlwise, make a yarn over, then knit the next two stitches together (knitting together the yarn over made in the previous row and the next stitch). Rep from * to the end of the row.

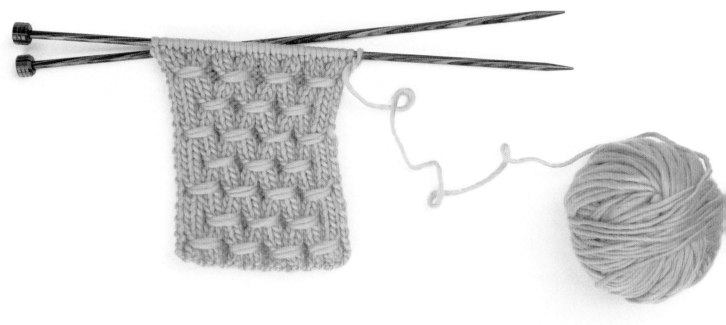

CLUSTERED STITCHES

This is a quick and easy way of creating a bold, chunky texture. You need a cable needle, and different numbers of stitches can be clustered together; here six are clustered.

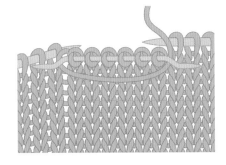

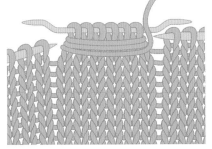

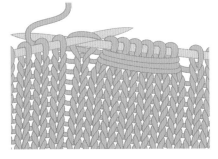

1 Knit across the stitches to be clustered, then slip those stitches onto a cable needle (see page 13). Bring the working yarn to the front and wrap it counterclockwise around the stitches on the cable needle.

2 You can vary the number of times the yarn is wrapped around the cluster; here, there are three wraps. Finish the wrapping with the yarn at the back, and adjust the wraps to lie neatly.

3 Slip the clustered stitches back onto the right-hand needle. Knit the next stitch to hold the wraps in place, then complete the row.

CLUSTERED LOOPS

These loops are worked on a wrong side row in stockinette (stocking) stitch, but appear on the right side of the fabric.

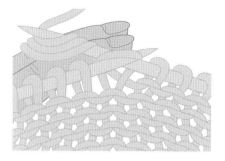

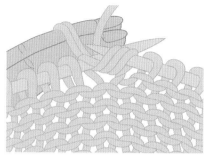

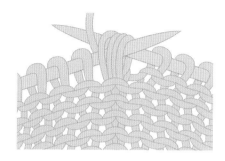

1 Purl to the position of the loops. Take the yarn to the back (right side) of the work and put the right-hand needle knitwise into the next stitch. Hold two fingers of your left hand behind the right-hand needle. Wind the yarn over the point of the right-hand needle, then over and around your fingers as many times as you want loops, finishing with the yarn going over the needle again.

2 Pull the loops on the right-hand needle though the stitch, without allowing the stitch to drop off the left-hand needle.

3 Slide your fingers out of the loops. Slip the loops from the right-hand needle onto the left-hand needle. Knit all the loops together with the original stitch as one, knitting through the back loops (see page 41). Pull the loops firmly down on the right side.

ELONGATING STITCHES

This technique creates a row of more open stitches. The effect can be emphasized by working this row in a different color yarn or wrapping the yarn more than twice if you wish..

1 Wrap the yarn as if to knit the next stitch, but instead of wrapping just once, wrap it over an extra time before working the stitch. Complete the knit stitch as normal, then repeat the double wrapping for each remaining stitch. It will now look as if you have double the number of stitches on your right needle. Turn.

2 Insert the right needle into the first loop on the left needle, as if to purl. Purl the stitch off, allowing the second loop to fall off the left needle as you push off the first one. Repeat for all other stitches. You should now have the original number of stitches again. Pull down gently on the bottom of the sample to stretch out the row.

The stitches in the row just worked will look longer than those in the rows below and may be a little looser. Garter stitch also works well with this technique.

CABLES

Cables involve moving groups of stitches, and you will need a cable needle (see page 13) thinner than the needles you are using to knit, to hold the stitches being moved. Work a six-stitch cable as shown here; for a four-stitch cable, just slip two stitches on to the needle and knit two, rather than three. For an eight-stitch cable, slip four stitches on to the needle and knit four.

CABLE SIX FRONT
This cable twists to the left and is abbreviated to "C6F" in a knitting pattern.

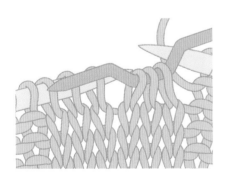

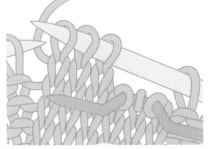

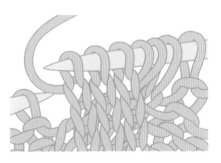

1 Work to the position of the cable. Slip the next three stitches on the left-hand needle purlwise (see page 61) onto the cable needle, then leave the cable needle in front of the work.

2 Knit the next three stitches off the left-hand needle in the usual way (see page 34).

3 Then knit the three stitches off the cable needle. The cable is completed.

CABLE SIX BACK

This cable twists to the right and is abbreviated to "C6B" in a knitting pattern.

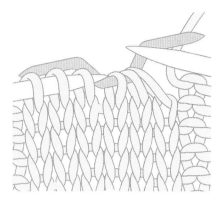 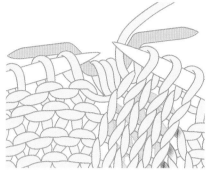 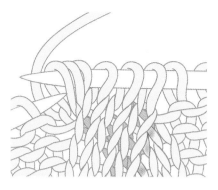

1 Work to the position of the cable. Slip the next three stitches on the left-hand needle purlwise (see page 41) onto the cable needle, then leave the cable needle at the back of the work.

2 Knit the next three stitches off the left-hand needle in the usual way (see page 34).

3 Then knit the three stitches off the cable needle. The cable is completed.

CROSSED STITCHES

When only one stitch is crossed over another, there is no need to use a separate cable needle. It can help to go up a size in knitting needles, because the yarn is required to repeatedly extend itself in the crossed stitches and so might lose some of its elasticity. Some textural patterns employ this technique.

BASIC CROSSED STITCH (WORKED ON THE KNIT SIDE)

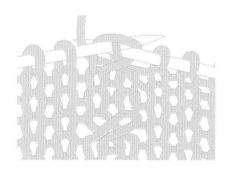

To cross two stitches, insert the right needle into the second stitch along on the left needle, going in from front to back. Knit this stitch, but do not push any stitches off the left needle yet. Next, knit the first stitch on the left needle, and then push both stitches off the left needle at once. You will see that a tiny cross has been created. Although very subtle, this pattern looks effective and pretty when repeated.

If you wish to cross on the purl side of the fabric, you simply purl the stitches instead of knitting them.

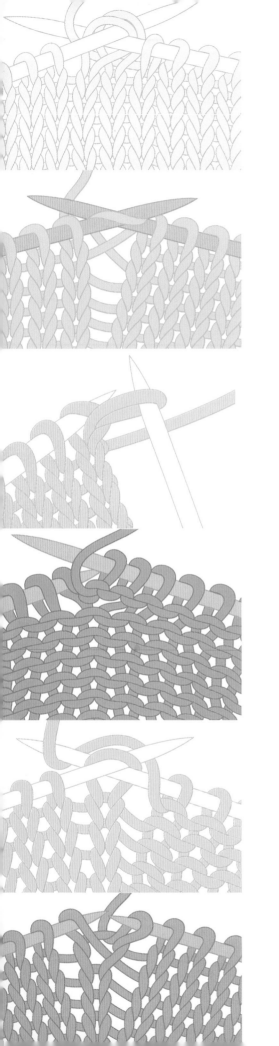

shaping

The process of increasing or decreasing stitches to shape the knitting is often known as shaping, and you may see this as a heading in knitting pattern instructions. It is usually separated out so you know when to begin working the increases or decreases. Decreasing and increasing are also sometimes used to create texture without changing the shape of the piece—in this case the number of stitches will be balanced out each time.

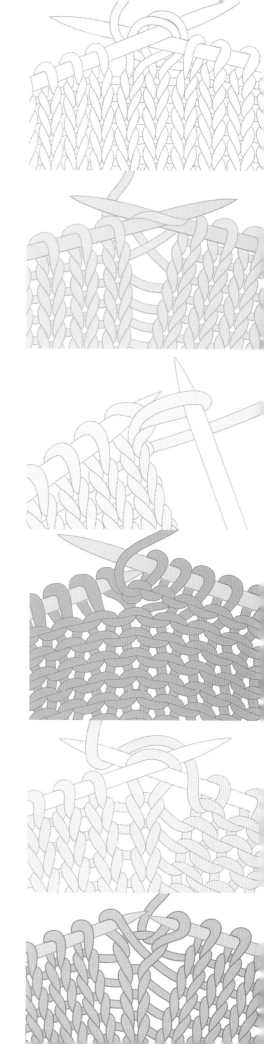

INCREASING

With this technique you create extra stitches to shape your knitting. There are several methods, which have variations depending on which row you are working on, and which direction the increased stitches need to slope in to create the effect you want. Your pattern will specify which method to use.

MAKE ONE LEFT ON A KNIT ROW

This method is usually abbreviated as "m1" or "m1l"—if a pattern just says "m1," this is the increase it refers to. It creates an extra stitch almost invisibly.

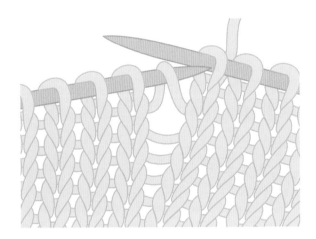

1 From the front, slip the tip of the left-hand needle under the horizontal strand of yarn running between the last stitch on the right-hand needle and the first stitch on the left-hand needle.

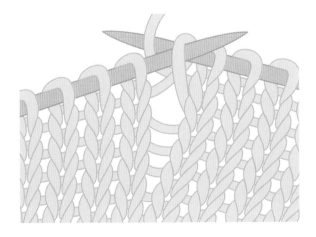

2 Put the right-hand needle knitwise into the back of the loop formed by the picked-up strand and knit the loop in the same way you would knit a stitch, but through the back loop (see page 41. You have increased by one stitch.

MAKE ONE RIGHT ON A KNIT ROW

This increase will usually be abbreviated as "m1r" in a pattern. It slopes in the opposite direction to "make one left on a knit row," opposite.

1 From the back, slip the tip of the left-hand needle under the horizontal strand of yarn running between the last stitch on the right-hand needle and the first stitch on the left-hand needle. Put the right-hand needle knitwise into the front of the loop formed by the picked-up strand, and knit it in the same way you would knit a stitch (see page 34). You have increased by one stitch.

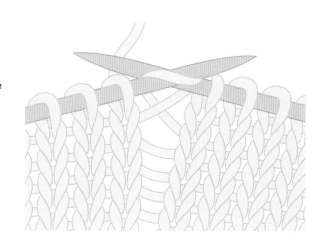

MAKE ONE LEFT ON A PURL ROW

You can also use make one increases on a purl row, and this version is usually abbreviated as "m1lp" or "m1p" in a knitting pattern.

From the front, slip the tip of the left-hand needle under the horizontal strand of yarn running between the last stitch on the right-hand needle and the first stitch on the left-hand needle. Put the right-hand needle purlwise into the back of the loop formed by the picked-up strand and purl the loop in the same way you would purl a stitch, but through the back loop (see page 41). You have increased by one stitch.

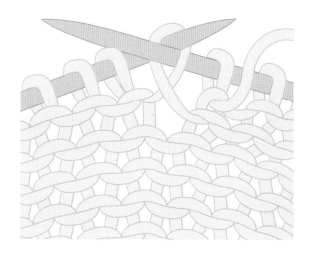

INCREASE ON A KNIT ROW

This is increase is abbreviated to "inc 1" in knitting patterns. There will be a visible bar of yarn across the base of the extra stitch.

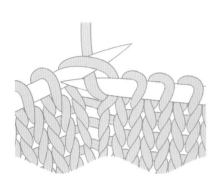

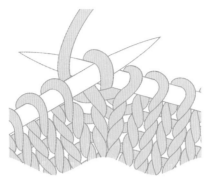

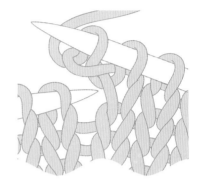

1 Knit into the stitch to be increased into as normal, but do not slip the old stitch off the left needle yet.

2 Knit into the back loop of the same stitch (see page 41 by inserting the needle from front to back, and then lift it off the left needle.

3 You should now have an extra stitch on the right needle. Continue knitting as normal.

KEEPING THE GAUGE (TENSION) CORRECT)

Try not to pull too tightly on the yarn as you work the increases, otherwise you will find them hard to work in the following row. To adjust the tightness if you need to, pull the right needle upward very slightly after each move and before slipping the stitches off the needles: this will take a little bit more yarn into the stitch, providing it with more flexibility.

PRACTICING INCREASING

To try out this increase method, you can work the following sample swatch.

Cast on at least 20 stitches, work a few rows in regular stockinette (stocking) stitch, then increase as follows:
Increase row (RS = knit side): K2, [inc 1, k1] to end.
Work 4 more rows of stockinette (stocking) stitch.

Make a second practice piece and create some increases in purl as described opposite, until you feel confident.

INCREASE ON A PURL ROW

You can also purl into the front and back of a stitch to increase by one stitch, though this can be a little fiddly to accomplish at first. This is abbreviated as "inc pwise." Again there will be a visible bar of yarn across the base of the extra stitch.

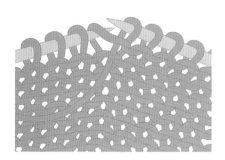 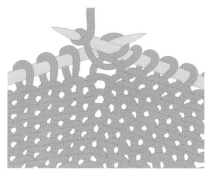 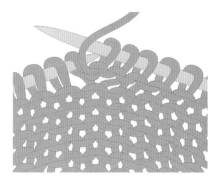

1 Purl the next stitch on the left-hand needle as normal, but do not slip the old stitch off the left needle yet.

2 Twist the right-hand needle backward to make it easier to put it into the same stitch again, but through the back of the stitch this time. Purl the stitch through the back loop (see page 41).

3 Slip the original stitch off the left-hand needle. You have increased by one stitch. Continue working as normal.

COUNTING INCREASE ROWS

You will notice that both these increases create a little "bar" at their base, where the yarn was brought to the front, and this can be very helpful when trying to keep track of your increases. For example, if you are knitting a sleeve you may see instructions to "increase one stitch at each end of every 10th row." There should be one of these tell-tale little bars at the edge of every row in which you have increased, so you can count the rows in between to ensure you are increasing on the 10th row every time.

FULLY FASHIONED SHAPING

When increases are made in a garment they are rarely worked on the very edge stitch, because this can look very messy. Instead, increases and decreases are worked on the 2nd or 3rd stitch in from the edge, which creates a much neater finish and is known as "fully fashioned" shaping.

MULTIPLE INCREASES

It is also possible to increase twice in one stitch, thereby creating two new stitches, using the same basic method—although this is a less common practice.

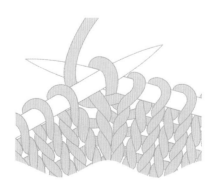 

1 Repeat steps 1 and 2 of the inc 1 method opposite, but do not slip the stitch off the left needle after working into the back loop.

2 Knit once again into the front of the same stitch, before slipping it off the left needle. You should now have two extra stitches.

MAKE ONE STITCH BELOW (M1 BELOW)

You can also make a stitch into the row below; this is abbreviated as "M1 below."

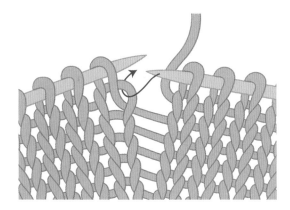

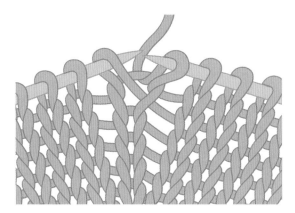

1 Find the top loop of the stitch below the next stitch on the left-hand needle. Insert the tip of the right-hand needle into that top loop from front to back. If this is difficult try picking up the stitch from the back, hold it with the left thumb and forefinger, then remove the needle and reinsert it into the loop from front to back.

2 Knit into the stitch, then knit into the next stitch on the left-hand needle in the usual way.

CREATING INCREASES EVENLY THROUGHOUT A ROW

Sometimes knitting pattern instructions may ask you to "increase X amount of stitches evenly throughout the next row"—it is particularly common in patterns with ribbing at the bottom of a front, back or sleeve that then changes to stockinette (stocking) stitch. This set of increases opens out the rib and makes a much neater transition between the two types of knitted surface.

Where to increase is very simple to work out—you just need to make sure all your increases occur at even intervals in the row—but there are some things to take into consideration. If you have 64 stitches and you have to make eight increases, you might initially think that you should increase one stitch every eight stitches. However, that would leave you increasing in the very last stitch, which is not a very neat soloution. Much better to work: "k4, inc 1, [k8, inc 1] 7 times, k4."

In cases where there is a difficult number of stitches to increase—for example, six increases over 64 stitches—you will have to use a little judgement. Use the method above, but add an extra stitch in at even intervals to accommodate those that do not fit neatly into the even distribution. In this second example, it would be best to work "k12, inc 1, [k10, inc 1] 5 times, k12." You have maintained even increases—and because the extra four stitches are at the edges of the work, they will be partly incorporated into the seams.

CASTING ON EXTRA STITCHES AT THE BEGINNING OF A ROW

If you want to increase several stitches at a time, the only way is to cast on stitches at the beginning or end of a row. This makes a more "stepped" increase, but in many cases this is appropriate. It is not as difficult as it might sound; it employs the cable method of cast on (see page 23).

1 Hold your needles and work as if you were beginning the next row as normal. Knit the first stitch, but do not drop it off the left needle yet.

2 Transfer the new stitch you have just created back onto the left needle, by inserting the left needle into it from front to back and from right to left. Then remove it from the right needle—this is your first new cast-on stitch.

3 To make your next new cast-on stitch, insert the right needle in between the first two stitches on the left needle, then knit a stitch; again, do not drop it off the left needle but transfer the new stitch back to the left needle, then drop it off the right one. Another new cast-on stitch made.

Continue in this way until you have made the desired number of new cast-on stitches.

CASTING ON EXTRA STITCHES AT THE END OF A ROW

Place the needle with all the stitches on it in your left hand, and work as if you were casting on stitches at the start of the next row, as described above.

CASTING ON EXTRA STITCHES IN THE MIDDLE OF A ROW

You may need to cast on extra stitches in the middle of a row, to create a 3-D effect, or as part of the construction of a buttonhole. To achieve this, work along the row to the point where you want to cast on the stitches, swap your needles over to use the one containing all the stitches just worked as your left needle, and then follow the method as described above until you have cast on as many stitches as you need. Switch the needles back around and continue as you were to the end of your row.

WORKING EXTRA STITCHES

Sometimes these extra cast-on stitches can be a little tricky to work on the first row, particularly when you are working with finer yarn. If you experience this, pull gently on the base of the cast-on stitch with your left thumb as you work it. This should loosen it up slightly and help you to slide your needle into it.

DECREASING

Another way to make a more complicated shape is by decreasing the number of stitches to make your work narrower. Again, there are several different ways to do this, depending on which direction you want the edge to slope.

DECREASES THAT SLOPE FROM LEFT TO RIGHT

Knit 2 together

The most straightforward of all the decreases, this simply involves inserting the right needle into two stitches rather than one, from front to back, and knitting as though they were one stitch. The top loop of the resulting stitch leans slightly toward the right, and therefore this technique should be used at the left-hand edge of the shaping, to create a slope inward from left to right. It is abbreviated as "k2tog."

Purl 2 together

You can also purl two stitches together in the same way: insert the right needle into two stitches instead of one, and purl them as if they were one stitch. This stitch also leans toward the right, creating a slope inward from left to right. It is abbreviated as "p2tog."

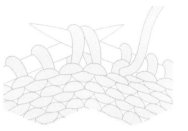

DECREASES THAT SLOPE FROM RIGHT TO LEFT

Knit 2 stitches together through the back loops

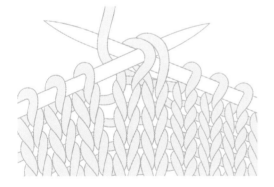

This is worked in a similar way to k2tog, but instead of inserting the right needle into the stitches from front to back, you insert it from right to left, through the back of the two stitches, and then you knit them together. It is a little fiddlier to accomplish but works well when teamed with k2tog to create symmetrical decreases, as it creates a slope inward from right to left. It is abbreviated as "k2tog tbl."

Purl 2 stitches together through the back loops

Sometimes you have to decrease to the left on the purl side. This is a bit more tricky to master, but this technique is the most common method to use. Remember, it will still show as a slant toward the left on the knit side, even though you have worked it on the purl side.

Starting at the back of the work, insert the right needle into the back of the next two stitches, from left to right. This will feel counter-intuitive but it is correct; the needle will emerge toward the front. Then purl the two stitches together from this position. Again, note that the resulting decrease slants to the left. It is abbreviated as "p2tog tbl."

Slip, slip, knit

This method is also quite a common way of creating a slope toward the left. It is abbreviated in patterns as "ssk."

1 Slip the first two stitches knitwise (see page 41) from the left to the right needle, one at a time.

2 Insert the left needle across the front of these two stitches, from left to right as shown, then knit them together.

Slip 1, knit 1, pass slipped stitch over

Yet another way of making a decrease that slants toward the left, and which can be used at the right-hand edge of the shaping. This is abbreviated as sl 1, k1, psso."

1 Slip one stitch knitwise so that you have a stitch on the right needle that is not knitted, but slipped. See page 41 for how to slip stitches knitwise.

2 Knit the next stitch on the left-hand needle as normal.

3 Insert the tip of the left needle across the front of the slipped stitch, from left to right, as shown, and lift it over the knit stitch and off the right needle, as if you had bound (cast) it off. You will notice that the resulting decreased stitch leans to the left, creating a slope inward from right to left.

Slip 1 stitch, knit 2 together, pass slipped stitch over

If you need to decrease by two stitches with a slope toward the left, work this method. It is abbreviated as "sl1 k2tog, psso."

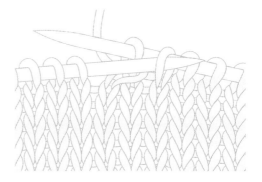

1 Slip the first stitch knitwise onto the right needle. Knit the next two stitches together as in k2tog (see page 58).

2 Lift the slipped stitch over the k2tog and off the needle, the same way as for sl 1, k1, psso (see page 59).

NON-DIRECTIONAL DECREASE

Slip 2 stitches, knit 1 stitch, pass slipped stitches over

Occasionally you may want to work decreases in the center of a piece, in which case you may wish to avoid any directional slant. You can only achieve this when working two decreases at a time. This method places the center stitch of the three that are worked together on top, and therefore maintains a straight look to the work. It is abbreviated as "sl 2, k1, psso."

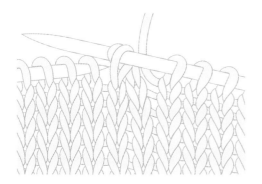

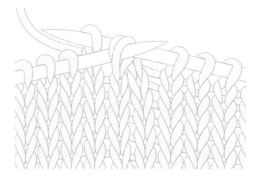

1 Work along the row as far as the stitch before the center. Insert the right needle into the next two stitches on the left needle, as if you were about to k2tog. Instead, slip them onto the right needle and do not knit them.

2 Knit the next stitch as normal, then lift the two slipped stitches over the knitted stitch and off the left needle. You should find that the center stitch lies on top of the decreases and has made a straight central column.

YARN OVERS

This technique is often employed to create a decorative hole or eyelet and forms a fundamental part of the techniques involved in lace knitting. It creates an extra stitch, so to compensate you will decrease a stitch to keep the same stitch count.

USING YARN OVERS

There are similar terms that can be very confusing: yarn forward ("yf" or "yfwd") refers to this technique when making a yarn over on a knit row; yarn over ("yo") refers to making a yarn over on a purl row; yarn round needle ("yrn") is when the yarn is physically wrapped around the needle to create the new stitch. The simplest way to compensate for the extra stitch made by a yarn over is to work k2tog or p2tog immediately before or after it.

Yarn over on a knit row
This is abbreviated as "yf or yfwd."

Knit 4 sts. Bring the yarn to the front between the needles, then insert the right needle into the next stitch and knit as normal. As you carry the yarn to knit the stitch it makes an extra strand on the needle, which you treat as a regular stitch on the next row. Repeat a few times across the row.

Work 2 rows in stockinette (stocking) stitch. The row of yarn overs just made should look like a row of decorative holes.

Yarn over on a purl row
This is abbreviated as "yo."

Purl 4 stitches. Take the yarn to the back of the work over the needle, then purl the stitch as normal. The extra strand created makes another stitch, which you should treat as normal on subsequent rows. Repeat another few times until you have grasped the technique clearly. End with a purl row, so you can practice the next move on a knit row.

Yarn round needle
This is abbreviated as "yrn."

Sometimes you need to make a yarn over in a pattern combining knit and purl stitches, such as ribbing or seed (moss) stitch. Simply bringing the yarn to the front or back will not achieve an extra stitch, because this move is part of the pattern, so you need to wrap the yarn fully around the needle. Bring the yarn forward all the way round the needle, ending at the front again; or, take to the back, wrap all the way round, ending at the back again. End with a purl row.

YARN OVERS AS INCREASES
Yarn overs are often made accidentally by new knitters, adding extra unwanted stitches. Avoid using themr as your chosen method of increase unless you are specifically instructed to do so—other methods are much neater.

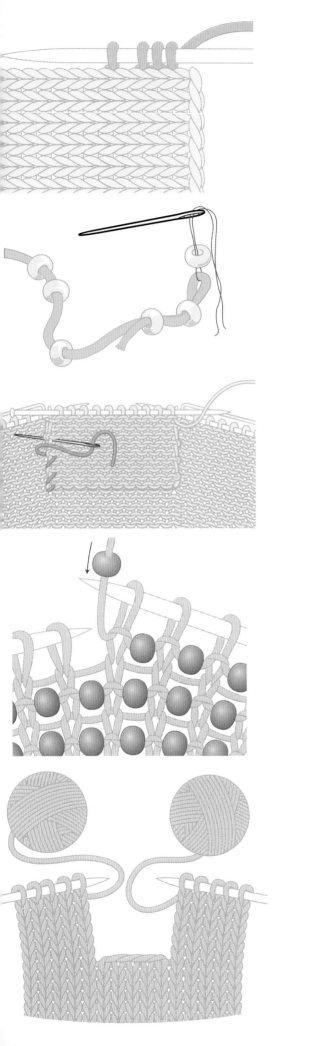

further skills

As you progress to more complicated items, you will need additional skills. This section covers holding and picking up stitches, as well as techniques such as making socks, adding buttonholes and pockets, and knitting with beads.

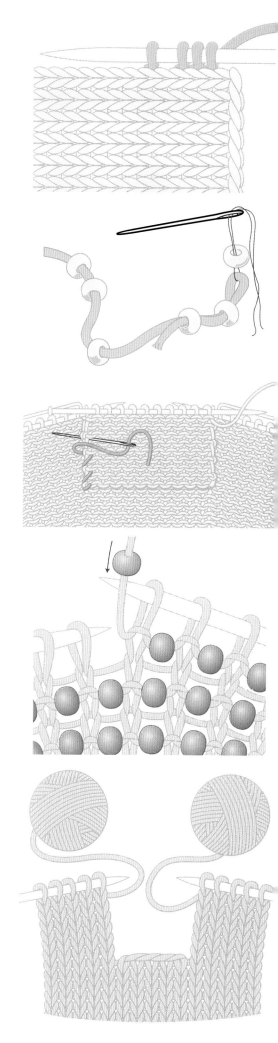

HOLDING STITCHES

The most common occurrence of needing to hold stitches is when creating knitted pieces that call for symmetrical shaping, such as when making a neckline in a garment. Because the neckline needs to be curved, it is not possible to knit it in straight lines—you have to knit each side separately. There are several ways to hold stitches until you need to work them, so you can choose which one suits a particular circumstance.

LEAVING HELD STITCHES ON THE NEEDLE

This technique is essentially to leave stitches not being worked on the needle until they are worked back into the piece. For some patterns, where the hold only lasts for a few rows—or when it is staggered and each stitch is held for one row longer than its neighbor—then this works fine. The stitches can withstand the extra tension put on them while they are held because it is not too substantial. Therefore for some projects leaving the stitches not being worked just sitting idle on the needle is fully acceptable.

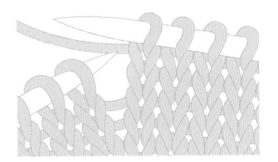

The method employed in these cases is to complete the first side, bind (cast) it off, then re-attach the yarn to the piece and complete the remaining side. You might also be asked to bind (cast) off stitches in the middle—this is straightforward and in this method should be done after working the first side so that the yarn is carried with you to the remaining side.

USING A STITCH HOLDER

Sometimes there are occasions when it would be inconvenient to leave the stitches on the working needle—for instance, when you have a very long piece to knit at each side, or if you are working an intricate pattern, perhaps with many colors. In both cases, as the first side piece is worked it will concertina up at the edge where you have held the non-working stitches. This will not affect the finished piece but it will make it difficult for you to check the piece as it is worked, and it will also become somewhat cumbersome if it is lengthy.

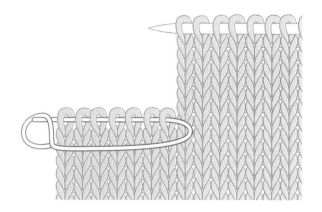

One solution to this problem is to slip the stitches that are to be held onto a stitch holder and remove them from the knitting needles temporarily. A stitch holder looks rather like a large safety pin: it has a straight bar for holding stitches and clips shut to secure them. Slip the stitches one at a time, purlwise, onto the bar of the stitch holder, then close it until you are ready to work them. Once you are, slip them back onto the left needle, again one at a time and purlwise, and work them as normal. If you only have three or four stitches to hold, a normal safety pin can act as a stitch holder, or you can even just thread them onto a length of thick yarn and knot it closed. This should only be attempted as an emergency measure and when you are very experienced, because transferring the stitches back and forth from the yarn without twisting them can be quite difficult.

WORKING TWO SETS OF STITCHES AT ONCE

The final option for holding stitches is not to hold them at all—instead you can join in a second ball of yarn and work the two sides concurrently, as separate pieces. To do this, work with the first ball until you reach the end of the first side, then drop it and take up the second ball and use that to work the other side. Turn the work, work with the second ball until you reach the end of that side, and then switch to the first ball again to complete the first side. The advantage of this method is that it ensures symmetry, because you make the same decreases and pattern details on each piece at the same time—and it can also be quicker. The disadvantage is that you must make sure the yarn does not tangle up—and multi-colored work would involve a second ball of each color used, which could quickly become very tangled.

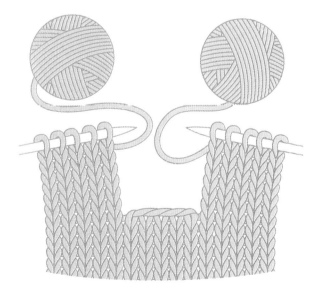

PICKING UP STITCHES

Being able to pick up and create stitches at various places within knitting is a great skill to learn. It offers scope for three-dimensional work and is a vital skill when tackling garments—it can help you create quite complex shapes, add edgings and borders, and knit pieces at different angles. If you eventually start to create your own knitting patterns and designs you can use this skill to avoid excess seams and produce very professional results.

PICKING UP STITCHES ALONG A HORIZONTAL EDGE

The phrase "pick up" stitches usually means "pick up and knit"; you may see that written out, or perhaps "knit up"—all three phrases mean the same thing. Essentially you are making new, active stitches from a completed edge. Whenever you pick up stitches you should never take the very edge loops, because this will look untidy, full of holes, and may become baggy. It is far better to take the next loop—or even the next stitch—inward, even though doing so may make for a slightly thicker seam.

The most straightforward way of picking up stitches is when you pick up the same number of stitches as there are in the piece, in a horizontal direction, and at the top of the piece. For example, if you are making a garment you will often have to pick up stitches from the top of the back piece when you knit the neckline: this will tend to be a straight line with one stitch picked up per knitted stitch of the piece. In such cases one shoulder may be sewn up first, with a given number of stitches in the center to be picked up for the neckline.

Picking up stitches along the top of a piece of knitting

First make a simple piece of knitting in stockinette (stocking) stitch, of at least 20 stitches and 20 rows. Bind (cast) off. Lightly press it with an iron so that it lies flat and you can see the edge stitches easily—this is one of the few times you will be asked to place an iron on the knitting!

Take a contrasting color of yarn and tension it in your hands ready to use. Hold the piece of knitting in your left hand, knit side facing you, and insert the right needle in through the center of the first stitch, directly below the bound (cast) off edge and not in the edge chain itself. Place the needle right through the central V. Wrap the yarn around the needle and pull back through so that you have created a new loop on the needle. Repeat for each stitch along the row (A). You should have picked up and knitted 20 new stitches, which are now active and ready to work with. If you were knitting a neckline, these would form your first row or round. Bear in mind that, if you wish to maintain the continuity of the

stockinette (stocking) stitch and have the knit side of the new piece carry on from the knit side of the old piece, then your first row worked will be a purl one using this method.

An alternative method for this type of picking up stitches includes using a crochet hook instead of a knitting needle (B), and then transferring the stitches back onto a knitting needle as you go along. This may be a useful skill to try when you have a spare moment, because very occasionally you might need to pick up stitches from left to right and this is far less counter-intuitive than using a knitting needle backward if you are right handed.

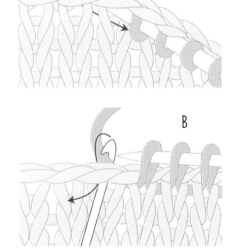

A

B

Picking up stitches from the center of a piece of knitting

There may be times when you wish to start creating a new piece of knitting from within an existing one, but not at the edge. For instance, if you decide to add a pocket in to a garment that is already finished, this is a possible solution.

Use the crochet method opposite, following along the row carefully. You might find it useful to thread a piece of contrast yarn along the row you wish to pick up before you start, to help you stay straight. Again, your first row will be a purl row if you are maintaining the flow of stockinette (stocking) stitch. Try it out on the test piece of knitting.

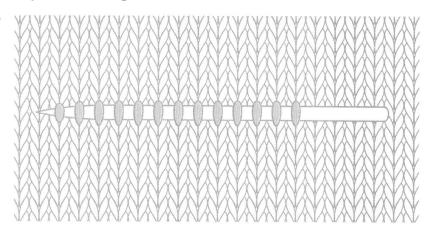

Picking up stitches from the bottom of a piece of knitting

This is relatively unusual but it does crop up sometimes. The technique of making the stitches is basically the same, but you turn the work upside down so that the bottom edge is at the top. The stitches are also effectively upside down now, so you must bear this in mind and treat the stitches as upside down Vs in order to be able to see where to insert your needle to pick up a new stitch. It will look as if you are working into the running threads rather than the Vs themselves.

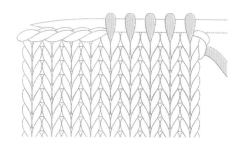

PICKING UP STITCHES ALONG A VERTICAL EDGE

This is another common technique, often employed to make button bands, along some necklines, or to edge blankets. It has an added complication in that you cannot simply pick up one stitch for every row, unless your pattern advises this, because knitted stitches are not square; the width exceeds the length. If, for example, the top and bottom each measure ⅜ in. (1cm) and the sides measure %₃₂ in. (7mm), a panel of 20 sts and 20 rows would measure 8 in. (20 cm) by 5½ in. (14 cm). So, if you picked up one stitch for every row along one side edge, you would pick up 20 stitches, which measure 8 in. (20cm) in

this example—but you only have a 5½ in. (14 cm) edge so you would have a very stretched-out distorted edge. Knitting pattern instructions will always tell you how many stitches to pick up along an edge—what you have to do is work out how often to skip a row when picking up to create a smooth edge. As a general rule, picking up two or three stitches then skipping a row will often produce the right number of stitches. In the earlier example you need 14 stitches over 20 rows, so you need to skip 6 rows in ypur pick up.

Picking up stitches along a side of a piece of knitting

Hold the piece with the knit side facing and rotated so that the bottom edge is on the right. Insert your needle into the running thread between the first and second stitches of the first row, and knit it up—this is your first stitch. Work along the same column of running threads, remembering to skip a row every three or four pick-ups, or as the pattern suggests.

When working this technique in garter stitch or seed (moss) stitch, you can pick up loops a little closer to the edge because the bumps on the purl stitches will not create such a visible seam as in stockinette (stocking) stitch.

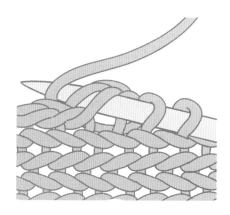

PICKING UP A DROPPED STITCH

However experienced you become, you will still drop a stitch from time to time. When spotted early it's easy to amend—but even if you don't see it for a few rows it's still relatively straightforward to put right. The best way to catch a dropped stitch early is to count your stitches often and regularly, and then you will see quickly if you have too many or too few. If you have too few stitches, look along your knitting for a loose loop sitting further back in your current row, or in the rows below—this is your dropped stitch. If you are not able to deal with it immediately, insert a stitch holder into it to prevent it from dropping any lower.

CATCHING A DROPPED STITCH IN THE CURRENT ROW

The best way to correct this is to carefully undo each stitch already worked on the row, one by one.

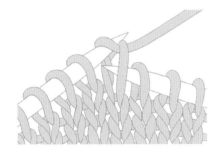

1 To undo stitches in a knit row, with right side facing insert the left needle into the stitch immediately below the one last worked. Push the stitch off the right needle and pull the yarn to free it. Repeat for each stitch until you reach the dropped loop. The principle is the same to undo stitches in a purl row, except that you work from the wrong side.

2 Pick up the dropped loop on the right needle and then the strand of yarn behind it from front to back. Insert the left needle into the dropped stitch from back to front and lift it over the strand, so that the strand becomes the new stitch. Make sure it is facing the right way and not twisted. Now work as normal to continue your row.

CORRECTING MISTAKES

The same technique of undoing stitches as shown above can be applied should you discover you have made a pattern or color mistake earlier on in your current row—simply carefully pull back each stitch, one at a time, making sure that each one is replaced on the needle without twisting it, until you reach the offending stitch. Pull that one back too, then re-work it correctly and continue your row.

CATCHING A DROPPED STITCH IN THE ROW IMMEDIATELY BELOW

This is a little different, but no more complex. Work the current row along to the point where the dropped stitch is sitting, so it would be the next stitch if it were actually on the needles.

On the knit side of the fabric

 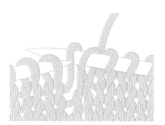 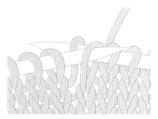 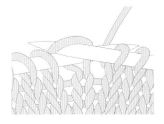

1 Make sure the horizontal strand of yarn between the correctly worked stitches is behind the stitch that has been dropped.

2 Insert the right needle into the dropped stitch loop, from front to back. Now poke the tip of the right needle from front to back under the strand of yarn behind the dropped stitch and lift this onto the right needle.

3 Keeping the working yarn tensioned fairly tightly in your right hand, use the tip of the left needle to lift the dropped stitch over the strand you just picked up, and off the right needle—just like a binding (casting) off motion.

4 Use the tip of the left needle to transfer the stitch you have just repaired back onto the left needle, poking it in from front to back.

On the purl side of the fabric

This is worked in a similar way, with just a few differences.

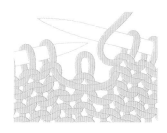 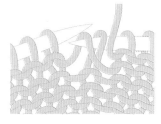 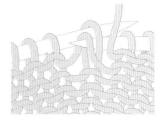 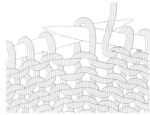

1 Make sure the horizontal strand of yarn between the correctly worked stitches is in front of the stitch that has been dropped.

2 Insert your right needle into the dropped stitch to catch it, but this time from back to front. Poke the tip of the right needle under the strand of yarn above the dropped stitch, from back to front this time, and lift it onto the right needle.

3 Keeping the working yarn tensioned fairly tightly in your right hand, use the tip of the left needle to lift the dropped stitch over the strand you just picked up, and off the right needle—just like a binding (casting) off motion.

4 Use the tip of the left needle to transfer the stitch you have just repaired back onto the left needle, poking it in from front to back.

KNITTING SOCKS

There are many avid enthusiasts of sock knitting, who always have a sock on their needles and who try out every possible method of creating these favorite items. And there are beginner knitters for whom the very idea of knitting with more than two needles is horrifying—if this is you, then look for sock patterns that are knitted on two needles and try those first. If you take your time and read the instructions carefully, you shouldn't have any problem creating your own knitted socks.

THE ANATOMY OF A SOCK

This diagram shows the various sections of the style of a typical knitted sock, and how the sections relate to one another.

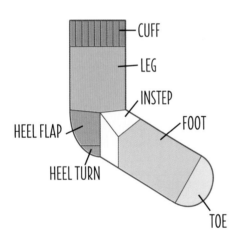

CUFF

LEG

INSTEP

FOOT

HEEL FLAP

HEEL TURN

TOE

TURNING THE HEEL OF A SOCK

This is the part of a sock pattern that causes most concern among non-sock knitters. The traditional method is to create two separate elements: the heel flap and the actual turned heel. The heel flap is worked on only a section of the stitches; the others are held on needles not in use. After the heel flap is completed, a smaller heel is turned on the same stitches; the terminology refers to changing the direction of the knitting so that the foot lies at a 90° angle to the leg part. Turning the heel involves decreasing this group of stitches on either side so that a small central group of stitches is then joined to the held stitches, to continue as the instep and foot section.

SHORT ROW SHAPING

This technique involves turning the knitting before you get to the end of the row. Normally you work along each row from the first stitch to the last stitch—but you do not have to do so. You can turn and work back again at any point in the row and this will make a shorter row within the piece—hence the term "short-rowing." If you do this over and over again, turning at specific points, you can create a variety of effects and shapes, from triangles and circles to ruffles and ruching. It is also an essential technique for socks, because this is how the heel and toe are "turned." The technique is essentially simple; the main thing to remember is to wrap the stitches at the end of each short row, whether they are knit or purl. The wrap ties the short row to the unworked stitch next to it, sealing any potential hole.

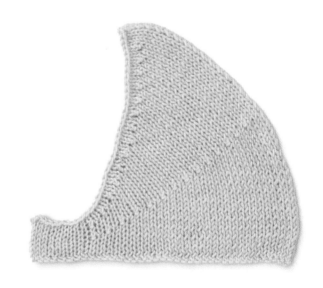

BUTTONS AND BUTTONHOLES

Buttonholes are usually worked horizontally, even when the button band is worked vertically. For the smallest buttonholes, working two stitches together with a yarn over afterward to retain the stitch count is sufficient. This will accommodate a small button or a bead used as a button. Larger horizontal buttonholes can be worked by binding (casting) off a few stitches and then casting them back on using a firm cast on method on the following row.

CHOOSING THE BUTTONS

Before working a set of buttonholes you need to choose the buttons. A good knitting pattern will give the diameter of the recommended button size, but some patterns are less specific. If you are devising your own pattern it's best to choose your button and then make a series of test buttonholes in a sample piece worked in the same orientation as the button band. The button should fit snugly but not too easily through the buttonhole, but bear in mind that knitting has a natural stretch and buttonholes used time and again will tend to expand slightly. So it is worth making a buttonhole that is initially somewhat tight, because it will eventually open up a little.

WORKING A STANDARD HORIZONTAL BUTTONHOLE

Cast on 10 sts, then work 10 rows in k1, p1 ribbing.
Buttonhole row: [K1, p1] twice, bind (cast) off 2 sts, [k1, p1] twice.

Next row: [K1, p1] twice, swap over the needles to place the needle containing the stitches you have just worked in your left hand. Cast on 2 sts using the cable cast-on method (see page 23), but before you place the last cast-on st back on the left needle, bring the yarn to the front. Switch the needles back to normal; [k1, p1] twice.

Work a further 10 rows in k1, p1 ribbing, then work another buttonhole as explained previously.

If you examine the buttonholes you have produced you will see that they are a bit flimsy; to reinforce them you can add a ring of buttonhole stitch (see below). Button bands are often knitted on a smaller size needle to retain tightness and neatness.

WORKING A VERTICAL BUTTONHOLE

It is possible to create vertical buttonholes, but they are slightly harder to work. You must work each side of the buttonhole separately, holding the stitches not in use, before joining the two groups together at the top, at the end of the buttonhole. This is a far less common method to use, and would be prone to stretching outward.

PLACING BUTTONS

Buttonholes and buttons do not have to be spaced out evenly. More creative options would be grouping them in pairs, with a larger space between each pair, or placing more buttons toward the top and fewer below, as on a smock. Consider the end use of the garment, and then decide on how to arrange the fastenings.

REINFORCING BUTTONHOLES WITH STITCHING

Adding an extra layer of firm stitching will increase the strength of a buttonhole; a simple blanket or buttonhole stitch works well, if the stitches are worked very close together, as in the diagram.

POCKETS

The simplest pocket in knitting is the patch pocket, which involves making the upper layer of the pocket as a separate piece of knitting, then stitching it onto the main piece afterward. A patch pocket is very versatile and you can decide on the design and where to place it after the item is finished, but it is not refined enough for certain types of garment. A slit or inset pocket offers a professional, neat finish that is more suitable for tailored garments.

SLIT OR INSET POCKET

This type of pocket is slightly more complicated to work, but with the help of stitch holders and a little patience it is worth the extra effort. Its disadvantages include that you need to plan ahead on where to position it and also decide on the size in advance; you knit the pocket inner as part of the main garment piece, so once it is made it cannot be changed without unraveling the entire piece.

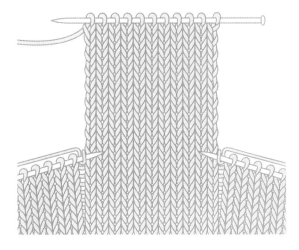

1 To try out this technique, cast on 30 sts and work approximately 10 rows in stockinette (stocking) stitch, ending with a purl row. Transfer the first 10 sts onto a stitch holder, then join in a new ball of yarn. Knit 10 sts then turn, slipping the last 10 sts onto another stitch holder. Now work 16 rows over the central 10 sts only, ending with a knit row. Fold the central strip of 17 rows over to form a pocket on the back of the work.

3 If you wish to edge the top of the pocket, then pick up stitches along the top fold of the pocket and knit across them, increasing by one stitch each end for neatness when you come to stitch the sides down. Work this border in a flat pattern such as garter, ribbing, or seed (moss) stitch.

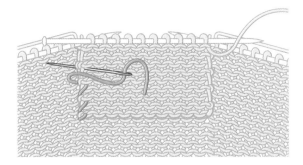

2 Place stitches on the left-hand stitch holder back onto the left needle and knit to the end. Turn. Work back across these last stitches and over the top of the pocket stitches, then place the stitches on the right-hand holder back on the left needle and knit these. Sew the pocket sides to the rear of the main piece using oversewing (see page 88).

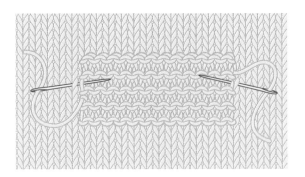

4 Bind (cast) off and then stitch the sides of the border down to the front of the knitting.

ADDING BEADS

Adding beads to a project is a great way to introduce pattern and texture, but the beads will add to its weight. Beaded knitting also tends to be wider than non-beaded knitting, so if you mix the two types of fabric you may need to increase or decrease stitches to adjust the difference. It's best to choose beads with holes only a little larger than the girth of the yarn, because if the holes are much larger the knitting will be looser and the beads will move about.

THREADING THE BEADS

You will need to thread all the beads onto the yarn before you start, or you willl have to cut the yarn to add more. If the beads are in a sequence of colours, thread the last one onto the yarn first, so that it will be knitted in last.

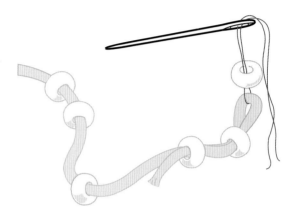

If your yarn is thin enough to accommodate the holes in your beads, loop the yarn through a small length of sewing cotton and then thread both ends of the cotton into a sewing needle. Push the beads onto the needle and then down onto the yarn in sequence. If your yarn is too thick then thread the beads onto very fine sewing thread and wind this back up into a spool. Knit the beaded thread together with the main yarn, to give the appearance of the beads being knitted into the main yarn..

KNITTING WITH BEADS

Once you have prepared your beaded yarn you are ready to start knitting. It is far, far easier to work with beads on purl stitches, or in a stitch pattern such as seed (moss) or garter stitch, because the horizontal bar of the purl stitch lends itself more easily to the addition of a bead. You can usually purl any stitches that have a bead attached, even if the unbeaded surrounding stitches are all knit stitches, because the bead itself will cover up any visible jarring of the stitches and hide the odd purl stitch.

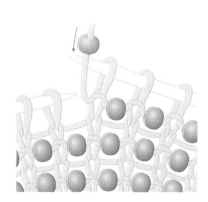

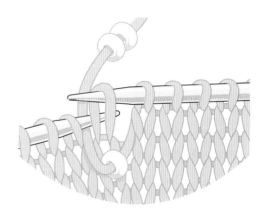

To add your beads, work as normal up to the first point where a bead is indicated. Work the next stitch, then bring a bead to the front of the work, and work the next stitch to secure it in position, ensuring that the bead sits on the front of the work.

It is possible to work beads into knit stitches but it is a lot harder to make sure they lie straight and even because the V structure of a knit stitch means the bead has to lie on one leg of the V. An alternative option is to slip the stitch behind the bead, as shown above.

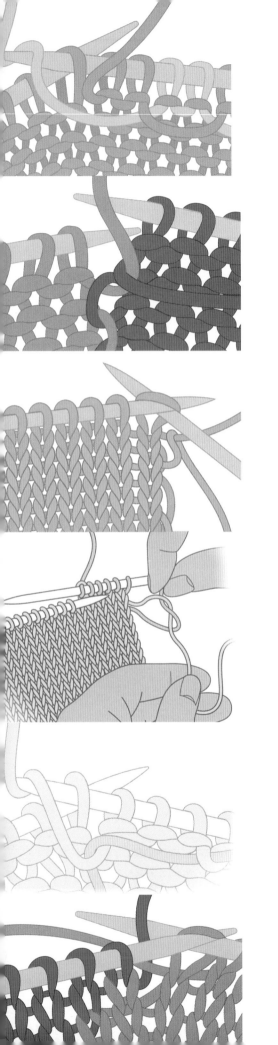

working with color

Yarn comes in a mouthwatering range of colors, and this section offers alternative techniques to use several different colors in your knitting, ranging from easy stripes to intarsia and Fair Isle. Intarsia is used to create large-scale color motifs and picture sweaters, while Fair Isle features lots of small repeating motifs, with each row worked in just two colours, building up to a complex-looking overall pattern.

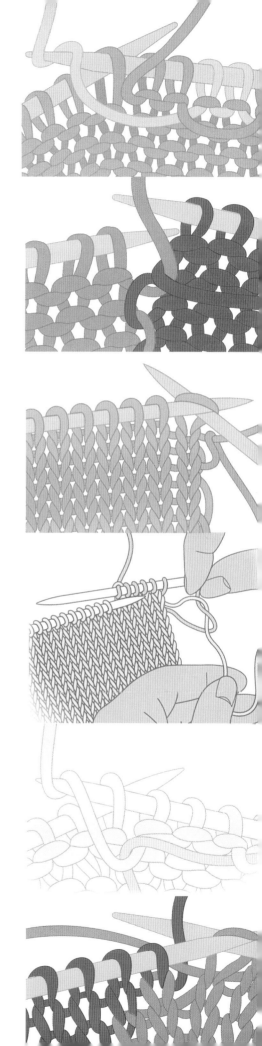

JOINING THE YARN

You will usually bring in a new ball of yarn or new color (as directed in the pattern or chart) at the beginning of the row/round.

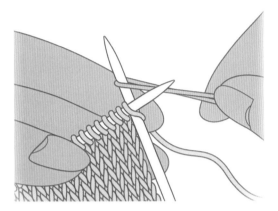

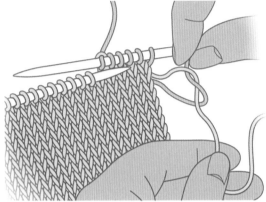

1 Break the old yarn, leaving about a 4–6 in. (10–15 cm) tail. Insert the needle into the next stitch to be knitted, then knit in the new color as usual, leaving a 4–6 in. (10–15 cm) tail.

2 The tails can be tied together to hold them in position and to stop the loose stitch from falling off the needle. It's best to knit one or two stitches before tying them in place. Never tie in a double knot, because this will make it difficult to sew in the end later and the knot will eventually work itself out of your work.

WORKING IN STRIPES

Stripe patterns are a lot of fun and are a great way to use up odds and ends, although take care to make sure that all the yarn you use is of a similar weight. It's also important to maintain an even gauge (tension)—if you work loosely you will create loose stitches at the edge and a messy appearance, and if you pull too tightly you will pucker your work at the edges.

JOGLESS STRIPES IN THE ROUND

A "jog" is created when knitting from one round to the next when the ends of each round don't stay lined up. As you knit up any item in the round using circular needles, you will notice that if you change colors at the beginning of a new round the color and/or pattern tends to fall out of alignment at that point. This is because when you knit in the round you are knitting a spiral, so the beginning and end of a round never perfectly meet.

To avoid this problem on stripe/solid sections, work the jogless stripe technique as follows:

Join in the new color in the first stitch at the beginning of a round and place a stitch marker. Finish knitting in the round to the end as instructed.

Commence the next round by picking up the stitch below the first stitch of the previous round (old color), slip the picked-up stitch onto the left-hand needle and knit together the slipped stitch and the first stitch of the next round.

CARRYING YARN UP THE SIDE OF THE WORK

When you knit stripe patterns you do not need to join in a new color for every stripe.
Instead, you can carry the color not in use up the side of the work until you need it again.

1 If the stripes change every two rows, then just bring the yarn not in use up and knit with it as needed.

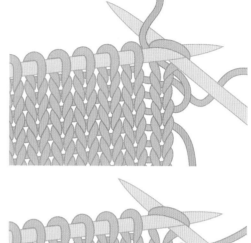

2 If the stripes are wider, then you will need to catch in the yarn not in use at the ends of rows to prevent long, loose strands appearing. To do this, put the right-hand needle into the first stitch of a row, lay the yarn to be carried over the working yarn, and then knit the stitch in the working yarn.

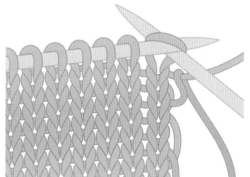

DIFFERENT EFFECTS

Always assess the qualities of both sides of a sample—you never know what you might discover. You may prefer the knit side, with its tidy appearance and bold stripes but sometimes a subtle change of color is required, as on the purl side. Here the stripes look very different, with thinner bands of color and uneven stripe widths.

COLOR KNITTING USING INTARSIA

Intarsia is method of color knitting used for motifs rather than for overall patterns. You need a separate bobbin or ball of yarn for each area of color. It's vital to twist the yarns in the right way to link the areas of color and avoid holes appearing in the knitting, so if this is a new technique for you, do practice on a swatch before starting a project.

CHARTS AND INTARSIA KNITTING

Using a chart for intarsia is incredibly helpful. Usually it will have colored squares representing the actual colors of yarn. So if you see 3 green squares next to 2 black squares, you know immediately to knit 3 stitches in green followed by 2 in black: it is an intuitive connection.

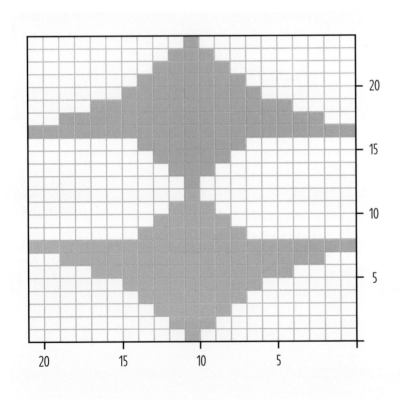

Working a chart

This chart is for an intarsia design: you can see that the rows and stitches are numbered, but the chart only shows the motif, not the whole item being knitted.

Typical instructions to position the chart would be:

Using A, k30(32:34:36), work Row 1 of chart to end; using A k30(32:34:36). Cont to work rem 23 rows of chart as set.

So for the second size in this example, k32 in yarn A, then work the first row of the chart, reading from right to left, beginning in the bottom right-hand corner and changing color as appropriate. Join in new balls of yarns B and A, work to the end of Row 1, then k32 in the second ball of yarn A to complete the row.

On the next row, p32 stitches plus the appropriate stitches in yarn A for Row 2 of the chart, reading from left to right. Change to yarn B where indicated, then back to the original ball of yarn A to complete Row 2, purling 32 stitches with that ball to finish.

Properties of intarsia

Intarsia is used to create large-scale color motifs, picture sweaters, or geometric designs and involves working with small balls of color and changing color within a row several times. The resulting fabric is only one layer thick (unlike Fair Isle or "stranded" knitting, which consists of the knitted fabric and a layer of threads at the back, see page 80).

PREPARING THE YARN

Before beginning, look at the chart to work out how many balls of each color you will need. Follow each row across and note how many color changes there are; each one will need a separate ball of yarn. Check all the rows, although as an area of color continues upward you can use the same ball of yarn as for the rows below. If in doubt, wind more separate balls because you can always use them later. To wind a small separate ball you can either use commercial yarn bobbins or

wind balls by hand. Commercially available bobbins have a slit in the top to stop the yarn from unraveling, which is useful for maintaining control when you are first getting used to the technique. To wind your own, first wind the yarn around your thumb and forefinger with you palm facing you, in a figure-of-eight motion. After this becomes full, remove the yarn from your fingers and wind around the center, making a butterfly shape.

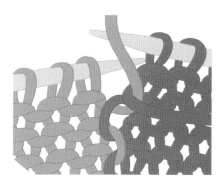 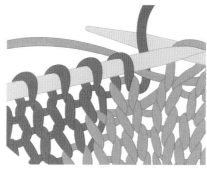 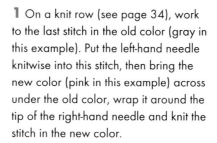

Vertical color change

Don't rush adjusting and linking the yarns on straight vertical color changes as the stitches can become loose.

On a purl row (see page 36), work to the last stitch in the old color (pink in this example). Bring the new color (gray in this example) from under the old color and purl the next stitch firmly. The same principle applies on a knit row. Work to the last stitch in the old color, then bring the new color under the old color and purl the next stitch firmly.

Color change on a slant

Where the color change runs in a sloping line, you need to be careful that the yarns are properly linked around one another at the change.

1 On a knit row (see page 34), work to the last stitch in the old color (gray in this example). Put the left-hand needle knitwise into this stitch, then bring the new color (pink in this example) across under the old color, wrap it around the tip of the right-hand needle and knit the stitch in the new color.

2 On a purl row (see page 36), work to the last stitch in the new color (pink in this example). Put the left-hand needle purlwise into the next stitch on the left-hand needle, then bring the old color (gray in this example) up under the new color and purl the stitch in the old color.

AVOIDING TANGLES

With this technique it's easy to acquire a mass of tangled bobbins on the back of your work, but there are ways of avoiding too big a mess.

First you need to accept that with this technique you will need patience, both in terms of following the charts accurately and in detangling the yarns at intervals.

If you are going to be working in the same spot for a while, try putting each little ball of yarn in a separate glass jar; they will be less likely to tangle and you will find it much easier to see how to detangle them.

Always twist the yarns in one direction when working right-side rows and in the opposite direction for wrong-side rows. This means you will be untwisting the initial twist when you work back.

FAIR ISLE

A lot of knitting that is called "fair isle" is not strictly Fair Isle in the true sense of the term. Traditional Fair Isle knitting employs lots of very small repeated patterns that only ever use two colors in a row. Knitting that employs more than two colors in a row is really stranded knitting—or jaquard, a rather old-fashioned term that you may see used in vintage pattern books. With intarsia, a separate ball of wool is used for each area of color; in Fair Isle, one ball of each color is used per row, and the yarn not in use is carried across the back of the work and picked up as needed. The strands or floats on the wrong side add an extra layer of wool behind the knitted piece, creating a really warm fabric.

FAIR ISLE CHARTS

Charts for Fair-Isle designs usually show a section to be repeated over the piece. In fact, there may be several different small charts, with each to be repeated across the whole row in sequence. With the small charts below, all the rows of Chart A are worked once in repeat across the whole width of the whole piece, then several rows of stockinette (stocking) stitch are worked before all the rows of Chart B are worked, again repeated over the whole width. Then a few more rows of stockinette (stocking) stitch, before all the rows of Chart C are worked, repeated over the whole row.

Then after a few more rows of stockinette (stocking) stitch the sequence begins again from chart B.

This is a common method of abbreviating charts; since the three patterns each have a different number of stitches, it would require a huge chart to show how they all fit together. Cutting each design down to a small repeat is also less daunting to follow.

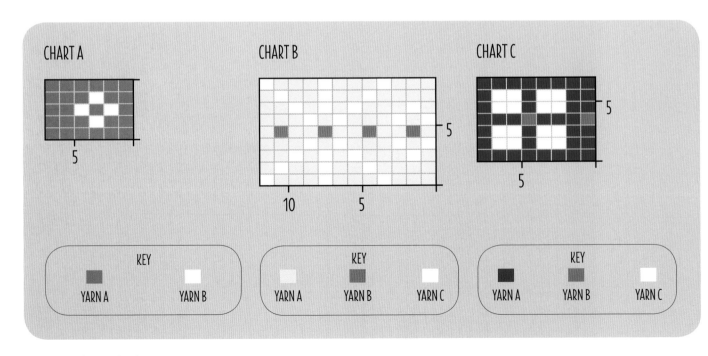

CHARTS AND SYMBOLS

In modern knitting patterns, colorwork charts are usually shown in color, with an appropriate color in each square to denote the yarn color you should knit that stitch in. With much older vintage patterns, however, you may find a black-and-white chart full of symbols rather than colored squares. If this seems confusing, and chances are it will, then make a photocopy of it and color the squares in using something light such as colored pencils, so that you can still see the individual squared lines.

FOLLOWING DIFFERENT SIZES ON A CHART

To follow an individual size in a knitting pattern you must select the appropriate number from a sequence, with larger sizes in parentheses, according to the size you are making; for example, "Cast on 20(22:24:26:28) sts." When a chart over the full width of a piece is given in a pattern with different size options, there will be a series of darker lines at either side, each one showing where to begin and end the chart for the particular size you are working. This can be another confusing feature if you are not conversant with following charts. Again, just photocopy the chart and either darken the lines for the size you are making and cross out the rest, or use a highlighter pen to color in the very last square of each row for the size you are working. This will give you a clear indication of where to start working the chart and where to stop. It also helps when you want to compare your work to the chart to check you have worked it correctly.

USING THE CHART

On the chart above right you would need to choose the right starting position for the size you are making from the options across the bottom, then work the necessary number of repeats of the center 5-stitch repeat for your size, then continue along to the appropriate end point for that size.

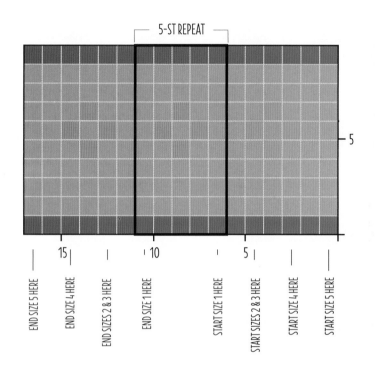

COMBINING FAIR ISLE AND PLAIN OR INTARSIA KNITTING

Fair Isle knitting has a tendency to be narrower than plain stockinette (stocking) stitch because of the strands running across the back. Many knitting patterns call for a blend of Fair Isle and plain knitting, but there will be a difference in gauge (tension) between these two types of fabric. To compensate for this, work the plain areas on a smaller knitting needle to bring the width of the plain knitting closer to that of the Fair Isle.

STRANDING

If you haven't tried Fair Isle knitting before, then it's a good idea to try it out on swatches before starting a project, as getting the gauge (tension) of the yarns right with the stranding can take a bit of practice. These instructions are for the simplest method of stranding, where you work holding one yarn at a time. You twist the yarns together before dropping one and changing to the next to avoid creating a hole.

Changing color on a knit row

It's important to swap the yarns in the right way when changing colors to keep the fabric flat and smooth.

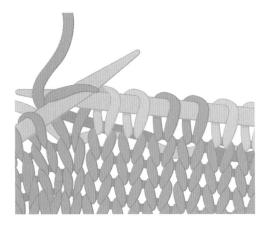

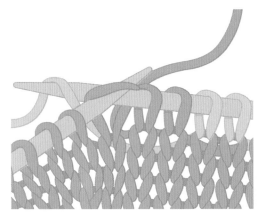

1 Knit the stitches (see page 34) in color A (brown in this example), bringing the yarn across over the strand of color B (lime in this example) to wrap around the needle.

2 At the color change, drop color A and pick up color B, bringing it across under the strand of color A to wrap around the needle. Be careful not to pull it too tight. Knit the stitches in color B. When you change back to color A, bring it across over the strand of color B.

Changing color on a purl row

You can clearly see how the colors are swapped when working the purl rows.

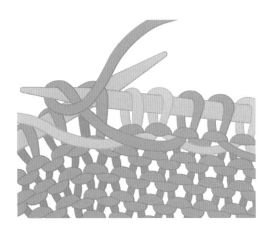

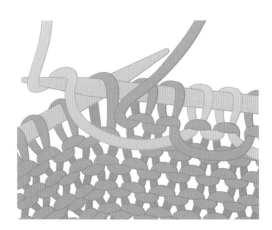

1 Purl the stitches (see page 36) in color A (brown in this example), bringing it across over the strand of color B (lime in this example) to wrap around the needle.

2 At the color change, drop color A and pick up color B, bringing it across under the strand of color A to wrap around the needle. Be careful not to pull it too tight. Purl the stitches in color B. When you change back to color A, bring it across over the strand of color B.

KEEPING THE STRANDS NEAT

When the yarns are swapped correctly, the back of the knitting is neat and tidy, with no loose strands that might catch and pull.

WEAVING

If the gap between color changes is more than five stitches—or as few as three stitches on thicker yarns—you need to weave the stranded yarns together at intervals by twisting them together. This technique is not to be confused with weaving in tails—to weave the yarns, they are twisted together on the back during the knitting, which shortens the loose float thread, making it much less likely to become caught.

To twist the yarns when working a right-side row

To twist the yarns when working a wrong-side row

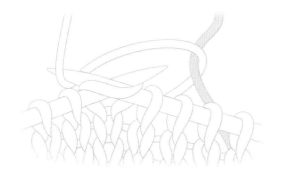

As with intarsia, try to alternate the direction you twist in to avoid developing great tangles on the rear of the work. You can either choose to alternate direction every other twist, or every other row. Weaving in should be applied when there are more than two yarns running at the back of the work. It becomes harder to manage the yarns as you work with more of them, so maintaining the gauge (tension) and alternating the twists is essential to keep your sanity. As with intarsia, Fair Isle knitting is not a swift process but the results are stunning. Once you become used to this twisting motion you can apply it to weave in yarn tails at the start and end of rows. Weave the tail and out of four to five stitches to secure it, thereby eliminating lots of sewing in at the end.

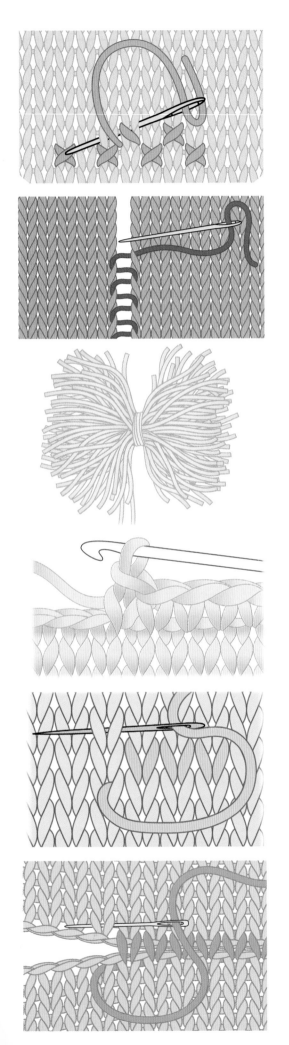

finishing and making up

The final touches to your knitted piece are to weave in any ends, join any pieces, and block the finished item to size and shape. After many hours of careful work, it makes sense to spend time on these processes to make your knitting look professional and well made. This section also includes some useful embellishment techniques.

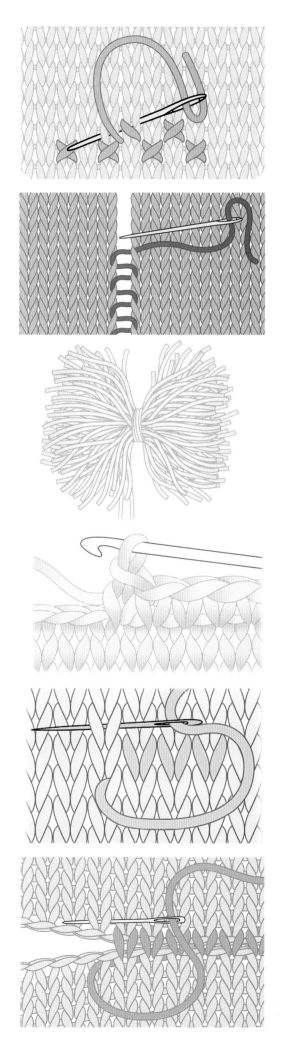

WEAVING IN YARN TAILS/ENDS

You may be able to weave in some loose yarn tails as you work, reducing the need to devote time to it at the end. However, there will inevitably be some to deal with when you have finished. This technique takes its name from the "weaving" motion worked as you sew the yarn tails in and out of the stitches on the wrong side.

EQUIPMENT

You will need a blunt-ended darning needle with a large eye—these are sometimes called "knitter's needles" or "yarn needles" and are often sold in pairs, one large and one smaller. A blunt-ended needle will not split the stitches into individual strands as you sew, which would make sewing much more difficult and produce a weak, untidy seam. You will also need small, sharp scissors.

KEEPING THE ELASTICITY

Be careful not too pull too tightly on the yarn tail as you work, or you will pucker the knitting and may reduce the elasticity of the knitted fabric. If it feels a little tight, stretch the knitting out a little and the yarn tail should adjust appropriately.

Where possible, try to weave in the yarn tails along seams, where they will be least visible. If you can't do this, then work as close to the seam as you can, and try to weave into an area of the same color as the tail.

Smooth and silky yarns need to be woven in for more stitches than coarser or woolen yarns, which have little hairs that grip and hold the tails in place. Working back on yourself as you stitch also helps stop the tails from slipping out.

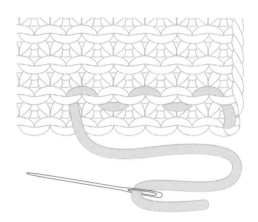

Take a yarn end and thread it into the needle. With the wrong side of the work facing you, follow along one row of horizontal stitch "bars"—this might be on the last/first row, or in the middle of the piece; wherever the yarn tail occurs, work in the row alongside it. Sew up and down through this row, working the yarn in and out so that it snakes through the stitches, as shown above. Work about 4 in. (10 cm) of the tail in, and then trim off close to the work.

BLOCKING

You will often see a reference in knitting instructions and patterns to blocking your work, which is a technique that allows you to adjust, straighten out, or re-shape your pieces before you sew them up. It is done after you have woven in loose yarn tails and does take a little time, but the results can truly transform the look of your finished item. Try to see it as a process that honors the amount of work you have put in, rather than a chore—it's like the icing on the cake!

The process involves dampening knitted (and also crocheted) pieces and pinning them out to the size or shape they are intended to be. It is particularly useful for achieving defined corners, accurate squares or rectangles, and to reduce the natural curl of some knitted fabrics. It is a fundamental necessity for items like fine lace shawls, which can look terrible when they come off the needles but are transformed into filigree works of art after blocking.

For larger pieces you will need a blocking board. You can buy ready-made blocking boards, but you can easily make your own, or you can use a regular ironing board.

EQUIPMENT

- Water spray bottle OR steam iron, depending on method/fiber
- Ironing board with a reasonably thick level of padding
- Steel pins—glass-headed or, ideally, T-headed quilter's pins
- Ruler and tape measure

BASIC BLOCKING

This method of blocking requires no specialist equipment. It is suitable for use with most yarns, and especially those that have a mainly natural fiber content. Before you begin, check the ball band of your yarn for the fiber content. If your yarn is acrylic, or a wool-acrylic blend, then follow the instructions for cold water blocking. If you have used wool, cotton, silk, or linen, then use the steam method.

1 Lay your piece of knitting flat on the ironing board and begin to pin in place. Beginning with the corners, if there are any, place the pins to hold the edge of the knitting firm without distorting it. Pin so that only the pin head is above the ironing board—the longer part of the pin should be under the work. Use a ruler or tape measure to check that each side is the right measurement. Ease out the knitting and adjust the pins accordingly until you have pinned the piece out to the right size. Make sure that any right angles are correct, and that nothing looks distorted.

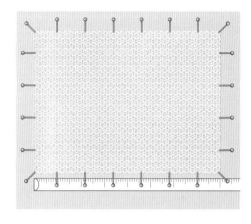

2 If you are using the cold water method (see introduction above) spray the piece with cold water, using the spray bottle, until it is damp but not completely wet through. Pat down gently on the piece to make sure the entire piece has become damp, then leave it to dry naturally before removing the pins.

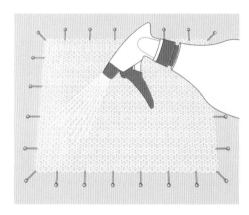

3 If you are using the steam method (see introduction above), set the iron to the correct temperature for the yarn you have used—check the ball band if you are not sure. Hold the iron just below 1 in. (2.5 cm) above the surface of the pinned-out piece and steam constantly for one or two minutes. Do not allow the iron to touch the surface of the piece, because this will ruin the texture and pile of the yarn and may create an unwanted shiny surface. Once you have finished steaming, remove the iron and allow the piece to dry completely before removing the pins.

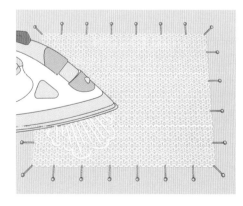

Repeat this for all the pieces of knitting you have prepared. In the case of small pieces, you may find you can fit several pieces on the board at a time, which greatly speeds up the process.

JOINING PIECES

After weaving in the yarn tails and blocking, all that remains to be done before your piece is complete is to sew it up. One of the simplest and fastest ways to join pieces together is by oversewing (also known as overstitching). It is not suitable for all joins because it is not as strong as some seams, but it is useful for joining smaller pieces. Other ways to join your pieces of work include backstitch, mattress stitch. flat stitch and kitchener stitch.

MATCHING THE SEAM TO THE PURPOSE

The most often used seams are oversewing, backstitch and mattress stitch. Here is an overview of each of these types of seam, detailing what type of seam to use where, and why.

Oversewing

Works well for quick seams, but is prone to pulling and does not look particularly neat—although if it is worked in a contrast yarn it can look very effective and decorative. Oversewing is useful when used with garter stitch because the thicker fabric disguises the stitches. It is also very useful for lightly basting (tacking) down edges. See below for how to work oversewing.

Backstitch

Best employed in seams where there will be a lot of tension and wear, such as shoulder seams and pillow seams. It does not work well in areas where fluidity with the drape of the fabric needs to be maintained, or where you do not want a bulky seam. Backstitch is a useful seam for children's clothing, which has to take a lot of wear and tear. See opposite for how to work backstitch.

Mattress stitch or fake grafting

Used when a hidden seam is desired— one that merges invisibly into the knitting. It is a very commonly used seam, suitable for use on ribbing, in the body of garments, sleeve seams, hats, socks, and multitudes of other purposes—a good all-rounder. See pages 90–91 for how to work mattress stitch.

OVERSEWING TO JOIN

This is one of the simplest methods of joining two pieces of knitting. It is normally worked with both pieces right sides together.

With both pieces right sides together and the edges to be joined aligned, take the yarn from the back of your work, over the edge of the seam and through the back again a short distance further on.

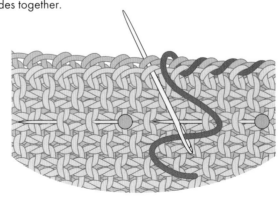

BACKSTITCH TO JOIN

Sometimes you need a seam that is more robust, stable and elastic than that provided by oversewing. In particular, the shoulder seams on sweaters or seams on heavier-duty items such as bags are generally worked in backstitch. This is because it can take more pulling, and therefore more weight being placed on it, than many other types of seam.

This stitch is worked in the same way as on woven cloth—you are always working back on yourself, hence the name "backstitch." You will see on the back that the stitches are much longer than those on the front and partly overlap each other—this is correct. Place both pieces right sides together, with the edges to be joined aligned. Pin carefully along, approximately 1 in. (2.5 cm) in from the edge. Try to make sure the pieces line up with each other with stitches corresponding—this is particularly important when there is any kind of texture or colored pattern in the knitting. Thread a blunt darning needle with a length of the same yarn or, in the case of a colored pattern, use the main color or background color.

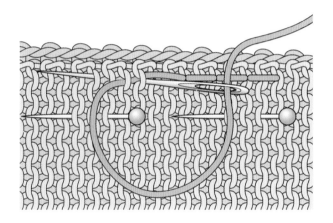

Insert the needle at the right-hand corner through both pieces of knitting and as close as you can get to the edge, from front to back. Bring the needle back through to the front one or two knitting stitches along in a straight line. Insert the needle back in the same space that you started, from front to back, and bring it back through to the front so that it appears one or two knitting stitches along from the end of the last stitch. Insert the needle at the end of the last stitch worked, from front to back, and bring it back through to the front so that it appears one or two stitches along from the last stitch. Repeat this to the end of the seam. Fasten off both yarn tails securely before cutting.

MATTRESS STITCHING ROW-END EDGES

The seam is worked from the right side and will be almost invisible.

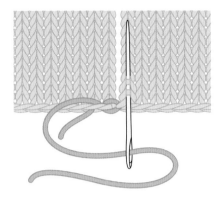

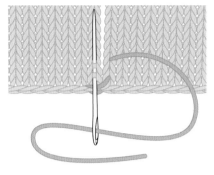

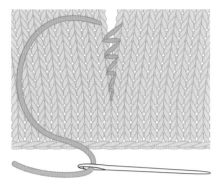

1 Lay the two edges to be joined side by side. Thread a yarn sewing needle with a long length of yarn. From the back bring the needle up between the first and second stitches of the left-hand piece, immediately above the cast-on edge. Take it across to the right-hand piece, and from the back bring it through between the first and second stitches of that piece, immediately above the cast-on edge. Take it back to the left-hand piece and, again from the back, bring it through one row above where it first came through, between the first and second stitches. Pull the yarn through; this figure-of-eight will hold the cast-on edges level.

2 *Take the needle across to the right-hand piece and, from the front, take it under the bars of yarn between the first and second stitches on the next two rows up. Take the needle across to the left-hand piece and, from the front, take it under the bars of yarn between the first and second stitches on the next two rows up.

3 Repeat from * to sew up the seam. When you have sewn about 1in (2.5cm), gently and evenly pull the stitches tight to close the seam, and then continue.

FLAT STITCH

Unlike mattress stitch, this stitch creates a join that is completely flat.

Lay the two edges to be joined side by side with the right side facing you. Using a yarn sewing needle, pick up the very outermost strand of knitting from one side and then the other, working your way along the seam and pulling the yarn up firmly every few stitches.

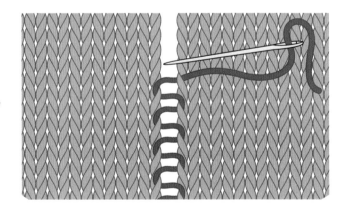

MATTRESS STITCHING CAST ON OR BOUND (CAST) OFF EDGES

You can either gently pull the sewn stitches taut but have them visible, as shown, or you can pull them completely tight so that they disappear.

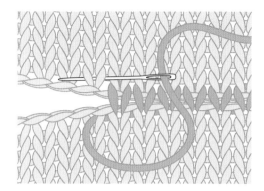

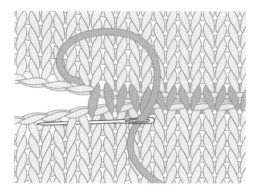

1 Right-sides up, lay the two edges to be joined side by side. Thread a knitters sewing needle with a long length of yarn. Secure the yarn on the back of the lower knitted piece, then bring the needle up through the middle of the first whole stitch in that piece. Take the needle under both loops of the first whole stitch on the upper piece, so that it comes to the front between the first and second stitches.

2 *Go back into the lower piece and take the needle through to the back where it first came out, and then bring it back to the front in the middle of the next stitch along. Pull the yarn through. Take the needle under both loops of the next whole stitch on the upper piece. Repeat from * to sew along the seam.

KITCHENER STITCH

This is also called grafting, and is used where you want to avoid a lumpy seam. It can only be worked on edges that have not been bound (cast) off, so you still have live stitches on the needle.

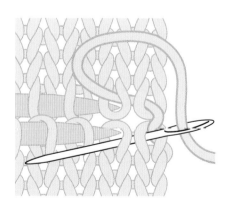

Arrange the two needles parallel with one another. Measure out the working yarn to four times the width of the knitting, cut the yarn and thread a knitter's sewing needle. From the back, bring the sewing needle through the first stitch of the lower piece and then, from the front, through the first stitch of the upper piece. Take the needle through the second stitch of the upper piece from the back, then from the front back through the first stitch of the lower piece. Bring it back to the front through the second stitch of the lower piece.

Continue in this pattern across the row, taking the sewing needle through a stitch from the front and then through the adjacent stitch on the same piece from the back. Take the needle across to the other piece of knitting and take it from the front through the stitch it last came out of, then through the back of the adjacent stitch on the same piece. Slide the knitting needles out of the knitted stitches as you join them.

FRINGED EDGING

There are a few ways to create a fringe, but this one is a tried and tested method.

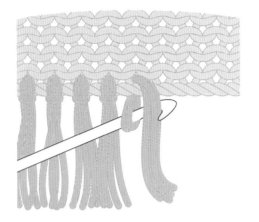

You will need a medium to large size crochet hook to complete this edging. Wrap the yarn around a small book eight times, then cut the end. Cut through the loops at one end so that you have eight short lengths of yarn. Fold two strands in half and insert a crochet hook into the loop to pull it through one stitch of the bottom edge of the knitted piece. Grab the ends with the hook of the crochet hook and pull them through the loops as shown. Pull to tighten.

Repeat these steps to add the remaining tassels of the fringe. You can place the tassels as close together or as far apart as you wish, and increase or reduce the number of strands of yarn in each to create thicker or finer fringing.

MAKING POMPOMS
BOOK METHOD

Use this method to make large pompoms.

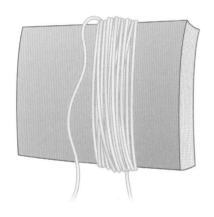

1 Leaving a long tail, wrap the yarn around a paperback book (or something a similar size) about 120 times, leaving a second long tail.

2 Ease the wrapped yarn off the book gently and wrap the second tail tightly around the center six or seven times.

3 Take a yarn sewing needle and thread in the second tail. Push the needle through the center wrap backward and forward three or four times.

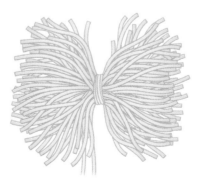

4 Cut the loops on each side of the wrap. Holding the two tails in one hand, hold the bobble and fluff it out.

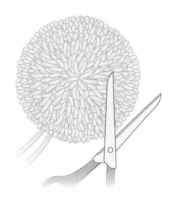

5 Hold the bobble in one hand and use sharp scissors to trim it into a round and even shape.

FORK METHOD

For small pompoms, use this fun method.

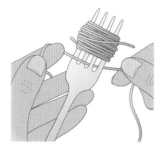

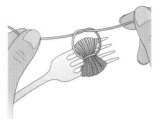

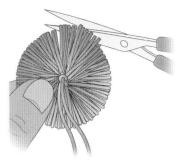

1 Keeping the yarn attached to the ball, wrap it around a fork about twenty times. Keep the wraps tight, and center them in the middle of the fork, leaving space at the top and bottom.

2 Cut the yarn and hold the wraps in place on the fork. Cut a 3in (7.5cm) length of yarn and thread it through the middle of the fork at the bottom from front to back.

3 Wrap one end around and back over the top until the ends meet, then tie them tightly together at the front. Wrap the tie around the center a few more times and tie another knot at the back.

4 Pull the wrap off the fork and pull the knot tighter. The wrap will begin to curl and turn flat and round. Tie a knot on top of the first to secure. Use sharp embroidery scissors to cut the loops on either side of the tie. Trim and fluff it up to a round, even shape.

CARDBOARD RING METHOD

This method can be used to make medium to large pompoms.

1 Using a pair of card rings cut to the size pompom you would like to create, cut a length of yarn and wind it around the rings until the hole in the center is filled.

2 Cut through the loops around the outer edge of the rings and ease slightly apart. Thread a length of yarn between the layers and tie tightly, leaving a long end. Remove the card rings and fluff up the pompom. The long yarn tail can be used to sew the pompom in place.

I-CORDS

You knit these cords on two double-pointed needles. The number of stitches can vary, depending on how chunky you want the i-cord to be, and a firm gauge (tension) works best.

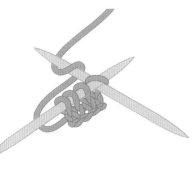

1 Cast on as many stitches as needed: here there are four. *Slide the stitches to the right-hand end of the double-pointed needle, with the working yarn on the left of the cast-on row. Pull the yarn tightly across the back of the stitches and knit the first stitch as firmly as you can, then knit the remaining stitches.

2 Repeat from * until the i-cord is the length you need. After the first couple of rows, it will be easy to pull the yarn neatly across the back of the stitches for an invisible join in the cord.

CROCHET CHAIN

An alternative way of making a cord is with a simple crochet chain.

1 Make a slipknot on the crochet hook (see page 22). Holding the loop on the hook, wind the yarn around the hook from the back to the front, then catch the yarn in the crochet-hook tip.

2 Pull the yarn through the loop on the crochet hook to make the second link in the chain. Continue in this way till the chain is the length needed.

CROCHET EDGING

A crochet edging can be worked along a horizontal edge or a vertical edge, but the basic technique is the same.

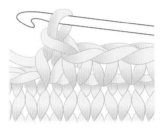

1 Insert the crochet hook in the first space between stitches. Wind the yarn around the hook and pull a loop of yarn through. Wind the yarn around the hook again and then pull the loop through to make a single chain.

2 Insert the hook through the next stitch, wind the yarn around the hook, and pull through a second loop of yarn.

3 Wind the yarn around the hook and pull a loop of yarn through both loops on the hook. Repeat steps 2 and 3, inserting the hook into the spaces between stitches in an even pattern. When working a crochet edging along a vertical edge, insert your hook into the spaces between the edges of the rows rather than the spaces between stitches.

EMBROIDERY

There is a range of hand-sewing techniques that can be used to embellish knitted fabrics after they are finished.

CHAIN STITCH
This is great way to add linear details or outlines. Bring the needle up through the fabric, then insert it in the same place and bring it up again a bit further along. Loop the end of the yarn around the needle tip before pulling through. This can also be worked as individual stitches in a circle to create a simple flower shape.

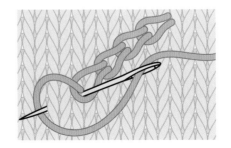
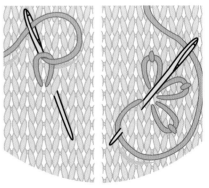

RUNNING STITCH AND STRAIGHT STITCH

Running stitch simply involves threading the needle in and out of the base fabric to create a line of stitches. Straight stitches are single stitches worked vertically or radiating outward. Try using thicker yarn than the base knitting, or a Lurex yarn that will glint in and out of the main fabric. Running stitch can also be employed to gather up finer knitting to create ruching.

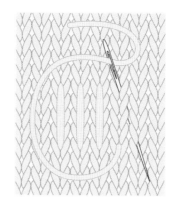

FRENCH KNOT

1 Bring the yarn out at the starting point, where you want the French knot to sit. Wind the yarn around the needle twice, or three times for a larger knot.

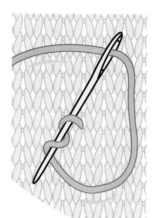

2 Take the needle back into the work, just to the side of the starting point. Gently pull the needle and yarn through the work and slide the knot off the needle and onto the knitting, pulling it taut. Then bring the needle out at the point for the next French knot or, if you are working a single knot, secure the yarn on the back.

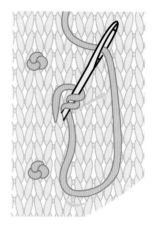

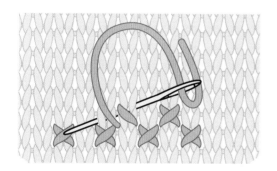

CROSS STITCH

This works very well because the diagonals of the cross blend well with the structure of knit stitches. Cross stitch works best on the knit side of stockinette (stocking) stitch, but it can also be worked reasonably successfully over a row of garter stitch or seed (moss) stitch.

SWISS EMBROIDERY

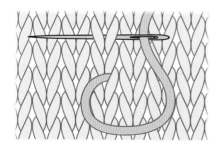

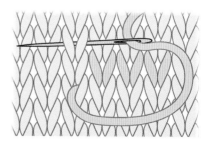

1 To work a horizontal line, start at the right-hand end. Bring the yarn out at the base of a stitch to be embroidered, then slip the needle around the top of the stitch, going under the "legs" of the stitch above.

2 Take the needle back through the base of the stitch and gently tighten the yarn so it covers the knitted stitch. Bring the needle out at the base of the next stitch to the left.

3 Continue to work along the row of knitted stitches in this way, covering each one with an embroidered stitch.

INDEX